W9-AGX-534

Phenomenological Hermeneutics and the Study of Literature

In the intensity of current theoretical debates, critics and students of literature are sometimes in danger of losing sight of the most basic principles and presuppositions of their discipline, of the underlying connections between attitudes to truth and the study of literature. Aware of this danger, Mario Valdés has taken up the challenge of retracing the historical and philosophical background of his own approach to literature, the application of phenomenological philosophy to the interpretation of texts.

Phenomenological hermeneutics, Valdés reminds us, participates in a long-standing tradition of textual commentary that originates in the Renaissance and achieves full force in the work of Giambattista Vico by the middle of the eighteenth century. Valdés characterizes this tradition as the embodiment of a relational rather than an absolutist epistemology: its practitioners do not seek fixed and exclusive meanings in texts but regard the literary work of art as an experience that is shared within a community of readers and commentators, and enriched by the historical continuity of that community.

Valdés demonstrates the vigour of the tradition and community he has inherited in a brief survey of such relational commentators as Vico, Juan Luis Vives, Wilhelm von Humboldt, Unamuno, Croce, and Collingwood. He elaborates the contemporary contribution of phenomenological hermeneutics to the tradition, referring particularly to the work of Paul Ricoeur. In arguing for a living and evolving community of criticism, he contests both the historicist imposition of closure on texts and the radical scepticism of the deconstructionists. And in readings of works by Octavio Paz and Jorge Luis Borges, he offers a model for the continuing celebration of the living literary text.

MARIO J. VALDÉS is Professor of Spanish and Comparative Literature at the University of Toronto. He is a Fellow of the Royal Society of Canada, and in 1986 was elected a member of the Mexican National Academy of the Language.

MARIO J. VALDÉS

Phenomenological Hermeneutics and the Study of Literature

UNIVERSITY OF TORONTO PRESS
Toronto Buffalo London

© University of Toronto Press 1987
Toronto Buffalo London
Printed in Canada
ISBN 0-8020-5718-7

University of Toronto Romance Series 56

Canadian Cataloguing in Publication Data

Valdés, Mario J., 1934–
  Phenomenological hermeneutics and the study of
  literature
  (University of Toronto romance series, ISSN 0082-5336)
  Includes bibliographical references and index.
  ISBN 0-8020-5718-7
  1. Criticism. 2. Hermeneutics. I. Title.
  II. Series.
  PN81.V34 1987   801'.95   C86-094717-3

COVER PHOTO Mario J. Valdés

'La secta del Fénix' / 'The Sect of the Phoenix' by Jorge Luis Borges, from
Labyrinths (copyright © 1962, 1964 by New Directions Publishing Corporation),
is reprinted by permission of New Directions.

This book has been published with the help of grants from the Canadian Federa-
tion for the Humanities, using funds provided by the Social Sciences and
Humanities Research Council of Canada, and from the University of Toronto
Women's Association.

To Anna Balakian, scholar, humanist, friend,
and once again to María Elena

Contents

Preface

This book was written between December 1982 and September 1984 as a companion volume to *Shadows in the Cave: A Phenomenological Approach to Literary Criticism Based on Hispanic Texts*. In the earlier book I examined principal issues of literary criticism from the perspective of phenomenological hermeneutics. These issues ranged from philosophical premises of criticism to methods of inquiry. There were, however, a number of basic questions relevant to my argument that I did not address directly, and these are examined here.

The first question pertains to the nature of the literary text itself. What is the text? Does it have a fixed or a variable identity? Is it shared by a plurality of readers? If there is a common ground for the reading experience, the next question is: What can we say or write about it that is other than a singular response and a personal reception? This discussion of the concept of intersubjectivity leads directly to a third question, the proposition that a shared meaning of a text is a reality in the world of action in which we live. The culmination of this discussion brings me to the examination of the ontological status of the critical text and its place within a community of readers.

Lest we be blinded by the intensity of the contemporary theoretical debate, we must be reminded that there is a long-standing tradition of relational commentary on texts that goes back to the Renaissance for its origins and attains full force with Giambattista Vico by the middle of the eighteenth century. The importance and significance of this tradition of commentators, which I trace from Juan Luis Vives to Hans Georg Gadamer, cannot be overstated, for there are still some critics who equate historical scholarship with the absolutist quest for author's intentions.[1]

This book is organized according to a basic tripartite plan: the tradition

of relational commentary, the argument for the assumptions of phenomenological hermeneutics, and the demonstration of the celebration of the
literary text through criticism rather than the historicist imposition of
closure or the endless deferment of the deconstructionist.

I wish to thank the various colleagues who invited me to read parts of
this book during 1983–4 and to express my gratitude to the many
colleagues who attended lectures and were good enough to discuss the
issues with me.

PHENOMENOLOGICAL HERMENEUTICS AND
THE STUDY OF LITERATURE

The units that we uncover by analysis signify nothing. They are simply combinatory possibilities. They say nothing, they are limited to conjoining and disjoining. But in the movement of going and coming between analysis and synthesis, the return is not equivalent to going. On the return, in ascending from the elements toward the entire text and poem, there emerges, at the juncture of the sentence and the word, a new problematic which tends to eliminate structural analysis. This problematic, proper to the level of discourse, is that of saying. The upsurge of saying into our speaking is the very mystery of language. Saying is what I call the openness, or better, the opening-out, of language.

You have fathomed that the greatest opening-out belongs to language in celebration.

Paul Ricoeur, *The Conflict of Interpretations*

PART I

The Philosophical Background

In this first part I am concerned with a fundamental bifurcation in the ways in which we comment on the world about us. The basic distinction is this: our considered view on the subject under scrutiny can be presented as a provisional statement, the best available to us at the time, one that is relative to our times, our learning, and, of course, our talent, or it can be presented as a proposition that purports to be a secure step forward on the road to truth.

This distinction in the ways of inquiry points out attitudes that are the embodiment of either a relational epistemology or an absolutist one. This is not a rigid either-or choice; it is more a general sense of purpose in the way we conduct our inquiry into reality.

In the following pages I shall examine a few of the high points of the relational tradition. Some readers will find my selection of writers wanting. If there were even the slightest pretence of writing a history of relational thought, I would certainly concur that the selection is deficient. I have limited my remarks to a rapid survey of those thinkers whose writing has come together for me in a coherent and highly significant tradition.

I fully acknowledge the importance and relevance of some of the writers I only mention in passing, such as Søren Kierkegaard, William James, John Dewey, and Ludwig Wittgenstein. And of those whom I do discuss, I do not claim that each of them was fully aware of the work of his precursors. There is no doubt, however, that Unamuno, Croce, and Collingwood felt a kinship that was fully acknowledged, primarily with Vico and in part with von Humboldt. These philosophers, although radically independent thinkers, come together on the fundamental metaphysical question of man's place in the world. They see man as engaged in a continuous process of world-making.

It is this position of relational philosophy from which I have consistent-ly taken my lead and to which I endeavour to contribute. Therefore, the task in this first part is to trace the historical development of an idea and to acknowledge the background to my own work.

There are two more tasks that are equally necessary for my theory: one is to establish the basis of critical verification not as adherence to an *a priori* principle but rather as a consensus of a community of commentators; the other task is to argue for a sense of purpose and responsibility in the critical commentary itself. I argue that it is because of the relational nature of human inquiry that we must look for authority in the consensus of the linguistic and cultural community. And it is because the purpose of writing criticism is to participate in the community that the critic is answerable to the community for his commentary as a factor in readers' redescription of their world. Therefore I consider the deconstructionist who advocates the giddy irresponsibility of a 'joy ride' to be just as misguided as the historicist who reaches for an elusive absolute truth. These two tasks must be postponed for the second and third parts of this book respectively.

1

Relational Theory from Vico to Reader-Reception Aesthetics

There is today widespread confusion about the nature of literary criticism, partly because nineteenth-century positivism has had such a pervasive influence on academic literary study in the English-speaking world and also because it has not been uncommon for academic critics, deluded by the purported search for definitive meanings, to have been more interested in self-promotion than in participation in the tradition of critical commentary that goes back to the *studia humanitatis* of the Renaissance. One of the most remarkable writers of the Renaissance was Juan Luis Vives, whose Christian piety was shaped into a pragmatic scepticism in the search for truth and, of even more significance, whose idea of fallible man did not deter him from accepting authority as a co-operative tradition in a constantly changing historical process. Because his writing is relatively unknown today, I would like to cite a few key passages. In his *De Prima Philosophia seu de Intimo Opificio Naturae* of 1531 Vives writes:

Penetramos en el conocimiento por las puertas de los sentidos; no tenemos otras, encarcelados como estamos en ese cuerpo nuestro. Así como aquellos que en una buhardilla no tienen sino una sola ventana por donde entra la luz y por donde miran afuera, no ven más sino lo que aquella abertura les permite, así también nosotros no vemos sino cuanto nos lo permiten los sentidos, aunque oteemos el exterior y nuestra mente colija algo más allá de lo que nuestros sentidos nos mostraron, pero hasta el punto que ellos nos lo consienten. Empínase la mente por encima de ellos, pero apoyada en ellos. Ellos le abren el camino y no le dejan otro escape. Colige que hay otras cosas, pero no las ve. Por eso, lo que nosotros decimos que es o no es, que es esto o aquello, que es tal o cual, lo conjeturamos del parecer de nuestro ánimo, no de las cosas mismas, pues ellas no son para nosotros la medida de sí propias, sino que lo es nuestra mente. Cuando decimos bueno, malo, útil, inútil, no lo decimos objetiva, sino subjetivamente. ... Por esta razón debemos nosotros juzgar de las cosas, no por sus características, sino por nuestra estimación y juicio. (2.1064–5)

We enter into knowledge through the doors of our senses; we do not have other means, imprisoned as we are in this body of ours. We are like those who live in an attic with only one window for the light to enter and through which to look outside; they do not see more than that one opening permits them to see; thus we also see nothing except that which our senses permit. Although we peek at the outside and the mind infers that there is something more beyond what our senses have shown us, even this extension is limited by what our senses permit. Our mind rises above the senses, but it is based upon the senses. Our senses show the way to the mind, and they do not allow the mind to escape them. The mind infers the existence of something, but it does not see it. Therefore when we say that something is or is not, that it is this or that, that it is such, these are all conjectures of our judgment and not from the things themselves, for they are not their own measure; rather it is our mind which is the measure of all things. When we say that something is good, bad, useful, or not useful, we do not say it objectively but rather subjectively ... For these reasons we ought to consider matters not by their physical characteristics alone but primarily on the basis of our own appraisal and judgment.[1]

If Vives holds to this scepticism of the capacity of fallible man to know anything with any degree of certainty, how can we engage so vigorously in critical commentary? The response that Vives gives is very close to the response that phenomenological hermeneutics gives to the radical scepticism of Jacques Derrida.

According to Vives, the limitations of man are insurmountable if he considers criticism to be an individual effort. Vives holds that it is only within the community of scholars through a co-operative undertaking of commentary that a temporary approach to truth can be made. And these truths will be revised again and again, subject to the constant historical process: 'eso lo daremos nosotros como verdad averiguada y reconocida por la generalidad del linaje humano' (2.1345); 'we will accept as true whatever is recognized as such by the totality of mankind.' But there must always be the critical scrutiny of all man-made constructs, for man is fallible since the original Fall of Genesis. Thus truth is reserved to God, and man in so far as he has been made in the image of God can strive for truth, but man's claims to truth are but temporary resting places in the unending inquiry into man's existence. The temporary nature of the truth-claim can only be bestowed by the community as a shared concept, but even this is with the full knowledge that it will be revised and changed as the community of scholars reaches a new consensus.

Juan Luis Vives was a Renaissance humanist whose thought, together with that of his famous contemporary Erasmus and others like Melanchthon, was part of a true international community of scholarship whose sense of open inquiry is the basis for the tradition of critical commentary that I have identified as the root of literary criticism. Vives himself used the word criticism to mean the judgment of argumentation. This is a view that is closer to our contemporary sense of hermeneutic commentary on the indeterminate writing of the imagination. Vives defined criticism in this manner: 'Esa parte de la Dialéctica llámase crítica con una voz griega, que equivale a decir juicio de la argumentación' (2.612); 'That part of Dialectic that is called criticism, with a word taken from the Greek, means the judgment of argumentation.'

The contemporary problem about the nature of literary criticism is also aggravated by an indifference to the philosophical presuppositions of criticism; this indifference makes critics and historians alike oblivious to a fundamental paradox posed by the stated aims of academic literary criticism and the presumed value of the literary work of art. On the one hand they pursue the quest for a definitive interpretation of the poem, play, or novel in question, but on the other there is the claim that the reading of the works of literature constitutes a valuable part of our aesthetic and intellectual heritage. E.D. Hirsch is a contemporary spokesman for this attitude, a development of the first half of this century; this quest for definitive meaning does not give the slightest recognition that if we accept a specific interpretation as definitive, we also render the literary text aesthetically sterile and worthless. This state of affairs has changed rapidly within the last two decades with the emergence of philosopher-critics like the late Paul de Man.

To my mind the arrival and success of literary theory in Europe and North America marks a coming of age of literary studies as a discipline. There is a maturity of a discipline that has the means to question and examine its basic assumptions, its procedures and claims. But to state that criticism has come of age with literary theory and that comparative historical study of works of literature is still the legitimate centre of activity and is fully compatible with literary theory is not good enough. It is necessary to take account of the tradition that begins in the Renaissance, gets new life with Giambattista Vico in the eighteenth century, and has been nurtured by a succession of philosophers, down to Hans Georg Gadamer and Paul Ricoeur in our own day.

Experience and common sense indicate that what we recognize and hold up as being true is nothing more nor less than what we have been able to make out from the massive array of data that life offers us. Beyond this general observation we can turn to a number of philosophers who have pursued this notion and have elaborated a philosophical generalization. The first philosopher whose work contributes to our discussion is Giambattista Vico (1668–1744).[2] The publication of his *New Science* in 1725 makes him the founder of the tradition of literary theory I wish to explore. This book is a remarkable breakthrough, for it cuts through centuries of writing that in one way or another sought to make truth an absolute quality to be assigned to certain data, the fundamental assumption being that what we perceive and experience is quite separable from our modes of perception and knowable in itself. Vico, however, postulates that when man perceives the world, without being fully aware of it, he perceives the shape of his own mind superimposed on the given data.[3] Therefore data can have meaning only in so far as the mind that perceives them has structures to cope with them, and the data that do not correspond to the perceptive structures will be dismissed as meaningless. Much can be said about the 'romantic' spirit of Vico's thought, that he extolled the belief that men created themselves, that man is the maker of the social reality in which he lives. But this line of discussion would only distract us from the key issue here, which is the foundation of a relational theory of literature.[4] The central point of Vico's work for this theory is the reciprocal nature of communication and specifically of language. Not only does man create in his own image, but his very creation in turn makes him what he is. Thus it is that man creates myths as modes of explanation; he creates institutions and traditions as means of continuation of his values, and in so doing he is in fact making the world, his world, which is a world perceived and constructed according to his talent.[5]

There is a common denominator in the multiplicity of world-making, and this is the deeply rooted need to enhance continuity; thus the world-making process consists of a constant repetition of forms. These forms are in fact heuristic devices that enable man to structure the given into a knowable, manageable conglomerate. The only danger in this process is that from time to time man confuses the man-made structure with the natural world, that is, with the given phenomenon of experienced data.

The New Science came to do battle with all truth-claims based on absolute *a priori* considerations of reality. The task was not one of finding favour with humanism over scholasticism or romanticism over rationalism; it was and is the rejection of any hypothesis proposed on a set of pre-existent, innate, and given facts. The two sides of the world-self coin are considered by Vico: the self as a member of a collective body of persons participates in the making of a social reality, each individual perception considered as a variant, and in turn the institutions, including language, are the principal instruments that influence the constitution of the individual's world-making process. Vico singles out the poetic capacity of man as his genuine distinctive talent, his distinctive ability to create. The *sapienza poetica* is the human talent to create world-views through myth, new meanings through metaphor, in general a redescribed world that has new significance for the recipient of the redescription. Vico suggests that there is a link between this human talent to create and the basic process of structuring the world that all men engage in as a matter of fact in everyday life, and he suggests that this link is the basic structure of man-made reality. The difference between the poet and his fellow men is one of focus. When we perceive the world in which we work, we do so in order to accomplish the task at hand. The possibility that what we construe to be given reality may in fact be an unconventional perception gets lost in the process because it is merely a means to an end as well as the means of our endeavours.

Another contribution in this historical line I am following came in the last quarter of the eighteenth century with the work of Wilhelm von Humboldt. Humboldt further extends Vico's relationist premise, for to the German philologist all study of language is based on the intimate unity of language and thought. He states that it is only because this unity exists that it is worthwhile for the philologist to make an abstraction of language as the object of research. Humboldt came to consider all languages as specific perspectives of the world, and it was on this basis that he set out to compare the various forms of languages as diverse as German and the non–Indo-European Basque. Humboldt's method was one of conscious abstraction of language in order to reveal its formal features.[6]

Humboldt held that the study of language brings out the means, but it is only in the use of language that there is the reality of the energy to communicate and to create. He developed his thinking on language by maintaining a clear-cut distinction between the abstraction of form and the reality of the individual's use of language. He wrote that however limited we may think the linguistic power of the individual is when compared to the potential power of language, there is a fundamental relationship between the individual's usage and the language, a relationship that allows him a certain creative freedom but that also restricts him. This freedom is limited in so far as every language has a view of its own over against *what* is said at any given time. One senses, he writes, the way in which the distant past is still connected with the feeling of the present, since language has passed through the sensations of earlier generations and has preserved their inspiration. Humboldt thus characterizes language as shared energy. He speaks of the individuality of inner meaning in the phenomenon of communication, and he explains this as the energy or power by means of which the inner sense of man acts on sound. Consequently language can be studied in its formal dimension, which can lead to an understanding of the flow of energy with which man knows and creates the world. This knowledge Humboldt called the historical life of the mind.

The next major contribution to the development of relational theory was the founding of synchronic linguistics by Ferdinand de Saussure in the early twentieth century.[7] Saussure also reacted strongly against the thesis that the material world consisted of independently existing objects that are available for precise objective observation and classification. With respect to language the objectivist position was that any specific language is the aggregate of the separate units gathered in the lexicon, and the whole of the collection has developed historically according to well-organized rules of linguistic change. Saussure rejected the substantive formulation of language in favour of a relational one. His thought can be summarized in four major postulates, each containing a dialectically related pair of concepts. The four postulates are: 1 / the mode of examination (synchronic-diachronic); 2 / the dimensions of language (*langue-parole*); 3 / the operational binary opposition of the system (*signifié-signifiant*); and 4 / the operational binary opposition of language usage, which later came to be syntagmatic-paradigmatic. The entire system is based on the initial abstraction of the synchronic status of language; therefore, it is of fundamental importance to examine the insight as well as the blind spots in the position he has taken.

Saussure's argument that language should be structured in terms of the relationship between the parts and in its present status as a functionally self-sufficient system is certainly in keeping with the broader intellectual rejection of reality as a conglomerate of given objects. But the essential failure in Saussure's formulation is that there is no means offered for establishing the relationship between the synchronic analysis and the diachronic record of change, and without this linkage the whole of the carefully constructed system of linear oppositions in postulates 2, 3, and 4 is open to criticism that it is based on an abstraction from reality, that language is a process and the validity of the analytical study is not applicable until it is reconciled with language as process instead of a frozen system. The theoretical problem has been resolved with the elaboration of the dynamic synchronics of contemporary theory, which is based on the concept of linguistic function.

There are four points I would like to make. First, the discerned structural properties of language must be taken as heuristic devices used for purposes of analysis, because they are based on an abstraction. Second, a distinction must be made between the consideration of language as a complex functional system of communication and any specific description of the system. Verbal communication is part of reality; linguistic description is an analytical attempt to isolate certain distinctive operational rules. Third, the philosophical tools that are needed are the means of reinserting analysis into the process of communication. And fourth, although Saussure states that *parole* represents the process while *langue* the system, this can be highly misleading, for though *parole* does focus on usage as distinct from the total system that serves as its ground, we must not lose sight of the fact that the fragment of actual usage has both a temporal dimension, which links it to diachronic consideration, as well as one of performance, which links it to the system. There is therefore a logical inconsistency in the basic premise of Saussure. If a synchronic analysis of language bifurcates into the consideration of the system as a whole (*langue*) and actual usage (*parole*), it is invalid because usage is always in time and its temporal dimension cannot be taken as mere supposition; that is, we cannot merely assume that there is a community of speakers who have developed their linguistic usage across time. The distinction between *langue* and *parole* can operate only if there is also a dialectical relationship between synchrony and diachrony.

Another writer of the early twentieth century who made a contribution to relational theory was Miguel de Unamuno; he is one of those philosophers who would qualify for inclusion in the company of the iconoclastic writers who have consistently challenged absolutes. Richard Rorty describes these writers with conviction:

On the periphery of the history of modern philosophy one finds figures who, without forming a 'tradition,' resemble each other in their distrust of the notion that man's essence is to be a knower of essences. Goethe, Kierkegaard, Santayana, William James, Dewey, the later Wittgenstein and the later Heidegger are figures of this sort. They are often accused of relativism or cynicism. They are often dubious about progress, and especially about the latest claim that such-and-such a discipline has at last made the nature of human knowledge so clear that reason will now spread throughout the rest of human activity. These writers have kept alive the suggestion that, even when we have justified true belief about everything we want to know, we may have no more than conformity to the norms of the day. They have kept alive the historicist sense that this century's 'superstition' was the last century's triumph of reason, as well as the relativist sense that the latest vocabulary, borrowed from the latest scientific achievement, may not express privileged representations of essences, but be just another of the potential infinity of vocabularies in which the world can be described.[8]

If ever there was a general description of Unamuno and the company he would like to be associated with, this is it. He would have added Vico and Humboldt to the list, and we would certainly add Croce, Collingwood, and Gadamer. Unamuno wrote his major philosophical essays in the first quarter of the century. Although he would live until 1936, he was never able to return to any of the basic issues of art and reality after his exile of 1926. In his writing he clearly acknowledged his debt to Vico and Humboldt, his kinship to Kierkegaard, and his appreciation of Croce, his contemporary.

In 1912 Unamuno wrote the prologue to the Spanish translation of Croce's *Aesthetics* of 1901.[9] I cite a few passages in order to feature both the Croce text and Unamuno's gloss.

La enemiga entre artistas y críticos creo que sea tan antigua como el arte y la crítica mismos, y el arte y la crítica son hermanos gemelos, si es que no son una misma y sola cosa vista desde dos puntos. Ciertísimo que todo verdadero crítico, si ha de merecer tal nombre a título pleno, es artista, y que reproducir una obra de arte exige a las veces tanto o más genio que producirla, y no menos cierto que muchos harían mejor que intentar darnos nuevas odas, pongo por caso, revivir ante nosotros las antiguas, las de siempre más bien, enseñándonos a gozar más y mejor de ellas. Pues criticar es renovar. Una obra de arte sigue viviendo después de producida y acrece su valor, según con los años van gozándola nuevas generaciones de contempladores, ya que cada uno de éstos va poniendo algo de su espíritu en ella. Lo más de la hermosura que sentimos al leer el Evangelio débese a la ingente labor de sus comentaristas, a las veces que hemos visto aplicada, cada una de sus sentencias. Y quién duda que el *Quijote*, verbigracia, es hoy, merced a sus críticos y comentadores, más bello, más expresivo que recién producido y virgen aún de lectores lo fuera? 'Sin la tradición y la crítica histórica–escribe Croce, el goce de todas o casi todas las obras de arte producidas una vez por la humanidad se habría perdido irremisiblemente; seríamos poco más que animales sumergidos no más que en el presente o en un próximo pasado.' (988)

13 Relational Theory

The enmity between artists and critics is as old as art and criticism themselves, and art and criticism are brothers, twins, if indeed they are not one and the same thing seen from two different perspectives. It is certainly true that every true critic, if he deserves the name, is an artist; the re-creation of a work of art demands as much if not more genius than it takes to produce one, and it is no less true to say that many writers would do better to help us relive ancient odes, enjoying them with us and participating more fully in the art of the ancient work, than to try to give us new odes. For to write criticism is to remake the work of art. A work of art continues living after the artist has produced it and grows in value in direct proportion to the years that it has been enjoyed by new generations of recipients, for each of these generations attaches some part of its artistic perspective to them. The greater part of the beauty we sense in reading the Bible is owing to the work of the commentators who have glossed all of its verses. And who doubts that *Don Quixote* is today, owing to so many critics and commentators, more beautiful, more expressive than when it was a newly produced virgin work of art. 'Without the tradition and historical criticism,' writes Croce, 'the enjoyment of all or almost all works of art produced by humanity would have been lost irredeemably; we would be little more than animals submerged in our present or our immediate past.'

In this passage Unamuno comments with approval on Croce's *Aesthetics* and adds his own exceptional views on the nature of literature, language, and, most important of all, the tradition of critical commentary. Many of the other philosophers I have drawn together as the relational school of thought elaborated the ideas expressed by Unamuno with more depth, with more extensive examples, but on all counts Unamuno was consistently a philosopher of relational reality.[10]

There are four major points that Unamuno is making here:

1 Art and criticism are one, the distinction being one of perspective. While the language of the poet redescribes the world, the commentator or the reader's reader who is the critic must also be capable of world-making in his commentary. The poet generates worlds; the critic regenerates them through his commentary. This does not mean that criticism and poetry are interchangeable; it does, however, further the concept that they both are but two different perspectives of the world-making process.

2 The role of the critic is therefore that of participation in the re-creation and expansion of the poet's text. *Don Quixote* is far more complex and a far richer work of art today than in the time of Cervantes. The traditional

didactic role of the critic is here abandoned in favour of the participatory and creative role as one in a never-ending series of commentators.
3 Unquestionably Unamuno is stressing that the aesthetic reality of art is in the reception of it. The poem transcends writing and the book and becomes a work of art in the reading experience. This aesthetic reality is not stable or permanent in any way; existence is one of dynamic process.
4 The most significant part of this passage is Unamuno's enthusiastic extension of Croce's idea of a community of commentary that spans the centuries and is the true author of the great works of literature that make up our sense of world.

This idea of the community as author is at the very core of the theory of phenomenological hermeneutics that I have examined in my book *Shadows in the Cave*, and it is this idea that I am placing at the centre of the present study. It is this central reality that, I believe, is absent from most post-structuralist theory. The realization that the text is indeterminate and inexhaustible need not lead us to a rejection of the collective and determining role of literary criticism.

Fueron y son los definidores los que infestan de pedanterías la estética y la preceptiva artística; son los que no logran acabar de comprender o más bien de intuir, que sólo se definen los conceptos, y que la expresión artistica, lo absolutamente individual y concreto, lo vivo es indefinible. El arte reproduce o más bien intuye individuos, y es muy exacta la observación que hace Croce de que Don Quijote no es sino el tipo de los Quijotes. (990)

The definers were and are the ones who infest aesthetics and poetics with pedantry; they are the ones who have not yet understood or, better said, intuited, that only concepts can be defined and that artistic expression, that which is individual and concrete, which is alive, is indefinable. Art reproduces or, better said, intuits individuals. Croce's observation is quite correct that Don Quijote is but the prototype of the [readers'] Quijotes.

This is one of the clearest examples of Unamuno's dismissal of normative poetics. The basic flaw in the aesthetics of those who subscribe to such poetics, he argues, is that they have forgot that all interpretative models and analytic tools are but heuristic devices to be used in the rational quest for understanding of abstractions. In short their error is to confuse their constructs with reality itself, to confuse their critical analysis with the literary work of art. The critical commentary does not stand in place of the work of art; if it is a shared commentary, it is added on to the prototype in the collective authorship of the literary work of art. Therefore, instead of a simplistic substitution of construct for prototype, Unamuno is saying that we have the prototype and the collective authorship, which with their cumulative force make up the literary work of art that the reader encounters.

Intuición es expresión; se intuye lo que se expresa, y el arte se compone de intuiciones ... Pero entiéndase que para Croce, la expresión es, ante todo, expresión interior antes de ser comunicada. A lo que conviene acaso añadir que nunca habría habido expresión interior a no haber la exterior, la que se comunica; que el lenguaje es, como el hombre mismo en cuanto hombre, de origen social. El pensamiento mismo es un modo de relacionarnos los unos con los otros. (991)

Intuition is expression; one intuits that which is expressed, and art is made up of intuitions ... But we should understand that for Croce, expression is above all the internal expression that precedes communication. To this we must add that there never would have been internal expression if there were not external expression, that is, communication; that language is like the human person himself in so far as he is human. Man is entirely of social origin. Our very thought process is but a mode of relating persons one to another.

This is a good example of the way in which Unamuno's gloss on Croce adds a specific dimension to the philosophy of language that Unamuno has taken from Humboldt. Language is the energy that transforms mankind from animals to persons. It is the collective social origin of language that gives the human being the capacity for thought and for aesthetic appreciation. Poetry is thus seen as a return to the very roots of being, for it is through poetry that the reader intuits his social origins. Other forms of writing, especially those whose abstractions lend themselves to absolutizing by the reader, are at the opposite pole from poetry that lives in the intuitions of the reader.

[Croce] niega el llamado bello natural, en cuanto algo independiente de la intuición humana. Para Croce, lo bello es la expresión lograda, *l'expressione riuscita*. (993)

[Croce] denies the validity of the so-called natural beauty, as something existing independently of human intuition. To Croce the beautiful is expression that has been realized, *l'expressione riuscita*.

Here Unamuno cites a key link between Vico and Croce, and he in turn gives it new life in Spanish criticism. It is this idea of man's remaking of the world, and especially his poetic genius for making the beautiful, that becomes the major aesthetic statement of expressionism in Spain. In writers like Gabriel Miró[11] the tie to Unamuno is clear and strong, but as is always the case, when a major concept becomes diffused through the intellectual life of a nation, it becomes the collective property of all. The Norton lectures of Jorge Guillén[12] give eloquent testimony to this fact in Spanish life, and the critical writings of Octavio Paz[13] do the same for Hispanic America.

La verdadera materia del arte literario, de la poesía, es el lenguaje que contiene en sí el tesoro todo de nuestras intuiciones. Expresar es nombrar. Se perciben los elementos materiales de una cosa, pero no se la conoce hasta que no se la nombra uno en sí. De que en una lengua falte el nombre de un objeto natural no se deduce que no existiera el objeto entre los que la hablaban, sino que no lo distinguían de otros, que no hablaban de él, que no lo conocían como tal. (995)

The true material of literary art, of poetry, is language, which contains the entire storehouse of all our intuitions. To express is to name. The material elements of an object are perceived, but the perceiver does not know the object until the perceiver himself names it to himself. If a name of a natural object is missing from a language, one cannot deduce that the object does not exist in the environment of the speakers of that language, but what is clear is that the object is not discerned and differentiated from others, that the speakers of this language do not speak about the object, that they do not know it as a separate entity.

I cite this Unamunian gloss on Croce in order to underscore the essential although generally unacknowledged ties that exist between Unamuno's theory of language and those of Edward Sapir and B.L. Whorf. The explanation is not difficult to come by: both Sapir (1884–1939)[14] and Unamuno (1864–1936), who were contemporaries but did not know each other's work, did share a common heritage in the work of Vives, Vico, Goethe, and Humboldt. According to Sapir, man knows the world through his language; according to Unamuno and Croce, man builds up his world-view through his participation in a linguistic community. The only difference is one of emphasis, from Sapir's anthropological concern with man's cognitive faculties to Unamuno's more metaphysical consideration of man's origin as a social being.

Sapir independently reached conclusions that reassert the proposition that an objective, unchanging, so-called real world does not exist. Vico's ideas of the reciprocal relationship between the linguistic community and the individual speaker of that language are restated by Sapir:

It is quite an illusion to imagine that one adjusts to reality essentially without the use of language and that language is merely an incidental means of solving specific problems of communication or reflection. The fact of the matter is that the 'real world' is to a large extent built up on the language habits of the group. No two languages are ever sufficiently similar to be considered as representing the same social reality. The worlds in which different societies live are distinct worlds, not merely the same world with different labels attached ... We see and hear and otherwise experience very largely as we do because the language habits of our community predispose certain choices of interpretation.[15]

Not only do we have Vico's concept of reciprocal relationship between the language group and the speaker, but we also have Humboldt's concept of languages as energy, as a continuum that creates as it goes along and then returns to the reservoir only to come forth again through the genius of the speaker. Let us be clear on the central issue here: Sapir is not saying that reality itself is relative, but only that our perception of it is relative. Each speaker experiences reality through a specific language, and since all natural languages carry a cultural code entwined, all speakers approach reality through the filter of a specific linguistic-cultural medium.

Once again the shadow of Vico crosses our path of inquiry as we come to the expansion of structuralism into anthropology. Not only is the ultimate aim the same in the writings of Vico and Lévi-Strauss – to create a general science of man – but also the fundamental axiom is the same, that men have made themselves to no less an extent than they have made the races of their domestic animals, the only difference being that the process has been less conscious or voluntary. Lévi-Strauss takes up the argument where Sapir and B.L. Whorf left it and extends it considerably. To Lévi-Strauss language is man's distinctive feature: it is the work of *homo sapiens* and it is also the means of all collective and individual creation. If man is language and language is society, could not the analytical methods of structural linguistics be applied to the study of culture? he asks, and French intellectuals responded. But the pitfall of confusing the constructed model with reality was clearly present.[16]

The structuralist principles developed in linguistics, when applied on a broad epistemological front by Jean Piaget and others, become fundamentally protodisciplinary formulations for a science of man. To summarize, Piaget's view of structuralism was based on the idea that, despite appearances, reality does not consist of independently existing objects whose concrete features can be perceived clearly and individually – that is, Piaget denies the existence of an empirically ascertainable world.[17] Indeed, the idea of relational reality holds that every perceiver's method of perceiving can be shown to contain an inherent bias that affects what is perceived to a significant degree. A wholly objective perception of individual entities is therefore not possible. The observer creates the world in his own image. Thus, the relationship that exists between the observer and what is observed itself becomes the central focus of study.

At this point it is important to note that the link and conflict between structuralism and phenomenology emerge in the context of the subject of perception. The early work by Merleau-Ponty 'Le Primat de la perception et ses conséquences philosophiques' and the major study *Phénoménologie de la perception*[18] challenged the structuralist notion of the closed system of language. This development, which would have been a much-needed corrective to structuralism during the 1960s, was unfortunately cut short by Merleau-Ponty's death in 1961. It would not be until Ricoeur's *La Métaphore vive* of 1975 that this position would be restated, but by that time structuralism would be in retreat before the sceptical forces of post-structuralism.

The immediate issue is to ascertain how the structuralist movement has a common source with relational theories. In brief, both structuralist and relational philosophers would agree that the state of affairs we refer to as reality has its existence bound not in things themselves but in the relationships that we construct and then perceive between them. Thus all structures are man's attempt to extend his domain. Vico's idea has thus attained a substantial following in the varied array of philosophers we are considering here. In essence the twentieth-century view remains true to Vico's dictum that the world is made up of relationships rather than things. At this point there is a major bifurcation in the development of that idea, between those who believe that there are permanent structures that in the last analysis must be structures of the mind – that is to say, the organizational categories and forms through which the mind is able to experience the world – and those who consider any structure to be a temporary heuristic device, useful in studying the processes of the real world. The latter writers are clearly within the tradition of relational theory.

As we approach the profusion of literary theories of the third quarter of this century, it is important to keep in mind that our purpose in this chapter is to draw attention to a common epistemological foundation that has so often been overlooked. A review of contemporary relational literary theory must begin with some commentary on the Russian formalists, who were the pioneers of critical self-reflection. The Moscow group was preoccupied with the techniques by which literary language works, and therefore they sought to specify and differentiate literary language from the modes of ordinary language. The group consisted of Boris Eichenbaum, Viktor Shklovskij, Roman Jakobson, Boris Tomashev-skij, and Jurij Tynjanov.[19] Although methods differed among them, their aims were the same: they were fundamentally concerned with literary structure. The work of art was *autonomous*, a permanent, self-determin-ing, continuous human activity that demanded nothing less than an analysis on its own terms and not as imitation. I shall summarize the contributions of Shklovskij and Jakobson. For Shklovskij the forms of the work of art are only explainable by the laws of art. His project was therefore to examine how literature was made and what literature was. But for Jakobson the subject of literary scholarship was not literature in its totality but *literariness*, that is, that which distinguishes a literary work of art from any other writing. It stands to reason, he argued, that the features will be found in the text and not in the author. By the same token, attention had to be given to the distinctive use of language and not to any particular topic.

The emphasis of the Russian formalists from their earliest work was on the study of the laws of literary production, which meant that when it came to literary analysis, attention would be on the *use* of poetic images and not on the presence of poetic images. Their work had unexpected fruits in the journal *Tel Quel*, which came to be a dominant force in theory of interpretation.[20] The starting point for the *Tel Quel* group was to reject the academic critical tradition of historicist criticism, which based the interpretation of literature on extratextual evidence. One of the points of attack was on the conventionalized use of genre and genre criticism based on historical data. The revolution in interpretation brought forward a series of new critical concepts: *écriture, intertextualité,* and *texte.*

The major thrust of *Tel Quel* theory was clearly linguistic structuralism in a new context, but ideological Marxism was soon grafted on to the new plant to produce a rather unique flora of criticism. In the words of Jean-Louis Baudry the aim of the group was to provide 'a theoretical activity whose purpose is to examine both the linguistic system, the transmission of information by which the social group speaks and lives, and the new formal systems of analysis that have appeared' (*Théorie d'ensemble*, 127).

What replaces the generic concept of the novel and theory of representation is *écriture* and its realization, *texte*. With this new orientation concerning the *signifiant* comes a radical concentration on the reading experience. In these first articles there was no concern with the moral intention so prevalent in the traditional criticism of the Academy. There was rather a focus on a new incompleteness of the act of reading.

When the only *a priori* given is language, literature becomes a system in which personal pronouns replace proper names, fantastic elements are neutralized, and there appear blanks in the text that function as areas of muteness of articulation around which the language pivots, in order to create a dense space in which experiences of dream, madness, repetition, and doubling coexist. *Texte* therefore replaces genre in theorizing. In opposition to the 'idealism' of a pre-existing meaning that is then expressed or copied, the text offers an open play of the *signifiant*. The text thus puts language into productive communication; this concept of *texte* can be seen as an extreme version of linguistic self-consciousness. The anagrammatic combinations, the 'polysémie,' the permutation of grammatical possibilities worked by and in the text in turn become the contribution of the reader. The text then is, in the view of Julia Kristeva, a translinguistic apparatus that redistributes the order of language through its production.

The choice of the term *texte* eliminates any suggestion of creation as the product of an individual personal effort. The text is not to be consumed; it has no market value; it is open, the property of all, a collective work of productivity. This, of course, is where the *Tel Quel* group's ideological stand enters. Much of the theoretical work of *Tel Quel* has been aimed at showing the close but subtle connection between the radical literary practice of writers like Mallarmé and social or political revolution – usually seen in Marxist, Maoist, or even Freudian terms. Their practical criticism seeks to bring about such a revolution of all value-systems – linguistic, economic, psychoanalytic, and political.

The basic idea that we encode the data of the world as the means of experiencing it receives a new lease on life through the work of Roland Barthes. There is no pre-formed world; there is no fixed reality; there is only a historically and culturally developed code of organization that constitutes our way of knowing reality. Consequently, in the tradition of Vico, Sapir, Whorf, and Lévi-Strauss we invent the world we inhabit. Like Don Quijote we modify and reconstruct what is given. Unamuno would only add the provision that we must recognize language as the primary encoder of experience.[21] It follows from this premise that no one has access to an uncoded or objective experience of reality, for it is clear that experience is always and by definition organized, that is, coded. Uncoded data are meaningless. This does not mean that specific institutions and generations of men from time to time have not promoted their particular code as reality itself. This state of affairs is what Roland Barthes with characteristic vigour has called the corruption of modern bourgeois society and its institutions.

If we now move to literature and literary criticism, Barthes's position is that all writing is a particular redescription of the writer's own view of the world.[22] Objective writing cannot exist. Writing is therefore misconstrued as communication in the sense that information is transmitted from speaker to listener. What we have is a set of particular views, more or less, flying under their own colours, being put forth as the world in which we live. Literature to Barthes is a highly conventionalized activity; thus, when a literary text offers a meaning, it also warns the reader that this is a view made up as a literary product.

Understanding is the fundamental relation of knowing one's self that underlies all experiential relations. Understanding is a process that begins with recognition and continues indefinitely as the infrastructure of experience develops and grows. It should then be emphasized that understanding in literary criticism is but a small part of the basic human condition. The difference between a literary text and the one not designated literary is just that the literary text gives extraordinary attention to the process of writing, which promotes strangeness in the text. Thus the initial encounter by the reader is one of alienation, which can be overcome only by a continuous effort on the reader's part. By the same token, the degree of ambiguity in the literary text ensures that the alienation will not be fully overcome. Each new reading will open up new possibilities. The living metaphor has the capacity to create anew at each encounter. If this situation is as Barthes describes it, are we locked into a fog-shrouded existence where certainty is impossible? If we were dealing with a static state, without taking into consideration the possibility of growth and common ground between readers, this would indeed be the case. The solution to the apparent impasse is the notion of temporary certainty, which is an integral part of modern science but woefully absent in historicist criticism. Barthes would have us proceed with confidence that whatever structures of understanding we construct will become obsolete with time but, in the best of cases, will have provided an important stage for an enriched environment of the collective experience of reading texts.

I would now like to turn to another aspect of contemporary theory, one that has not gone through the structuralist and post-structuralist adventure: reader-reception theory. This theory has an important place among contemporary theories of interpretation. Its main attraction has been its functional orientation, which is readily transmitted into practical criticism. The foremost centre of research has been the University of Constance in Germany, and the leading proponents are Wolfgang Iser and Hans Robert Jauss, both former students of Hans Georg Gadamer and both influenced by phenomenological philosophy. Although there are differences between the various positions that have been taken, the common ground is clear. Iser states it succinctly: 'The phenomenological theory of art lays full stress on the idea that, in considering a literary work, one must take into account not only the actual text but also in equal measure, the action involved in responding to the text.'[23] Those critics who identify themselves with reader-reception theory agree on the basic distinction between the literary work of art and the text. The text being only potentially meaningful, its potential is realized only when a reader actualizes the text in reading. The influence of Gadamer is evident in the premise that the actualization by the reader involves the full range of the reader's disposition. Iser's theoretical focus has been on the different patterns in the text that solicit specific modes of response from the reader. Thus Iser's area of concern is the interaction between text and reader. Jauss, meanwhile, has stressed the collective aspects of the reader's predisposition to the text.[24]

Reader-reception theory, largely through the efforts of the Constance school, has become one of the most clearly articulated theories within the tradition of the Viconean revolution, buttressed as it is today by the philosophy of Husserl, Heidegger, Gadamer, Ingarden, and more recently Ricoeur. The ties between my theoretical position and that of the reception-aesthetics scholars at Constance are evidently strong and markedly interdependent. This is so primarily because of common points of departure in the work of Heidegger, Ingarden, Gadamer, Merleau-Ponty, and Ricoeur, but also because of more than fifteen years of collaboration, going back to 1972, when Wolfgang Iser taught at Toronto, and the 1974 colloquium on narrative, which culminated in *Interpretation of Narrative*, in which both Iser and Hans Robert Jauss took part. This was followed with the full participation of both German scholars in *Identity of the Literary Text* (1985), which highlighted a firmly established involvement of Constance and Toronto over the intervening years.

It is, however, important to make some distinctions between the Constance school and phenomenological hermeneutics. The principal difference is in the scope of the theory. While my theory of phenomenological hermeneutics stresses the broadest scope of operation in criticism, ranging from the pre-figurative cultural well-spring of texts to the configurative level of organization and composition and concluding with the refiguration of the text by the reader, my colleagues at Constance have a sharper focus and concentrate on specific areas within the spectrum I discuss. Hans Robert Jauss has given his major attention to the interaction between society and text – that is, in my terms, to the relationship between the pre-figurative and the configurative dimensions of the text. Wolfgang Iser has scrutinized the text-reader relationship with extraordinary rigour; this relationship corresponds to the movement from the configurative to the refigurative dimension of the text in my theory. Thus it is that I consider our work to be complementary. What my theory lacks in sharp focus is completely overcome by the work of my German colleagues.

I have attempted to trace the development of a diversity of theoretical approaches that stem from Vico's relational claims for man as world-maker. This same thinker is generally acknowledged as the founder of modern philology, upon which comparative literary history ultimately depends for its disciplinary presuppositions. Vico's stand against Cartesian philosophy led him to single out the creative dimension of man as a primary area of study and as a distinctive kind of knowledge. The old Aristotelian distinction between practical and theoretical knowledge is taken once again. This is a distinction that cannot be reduced to the quest for truth as separate from the probable. Practical knowledge, *phronesis,* is another kind of knowledge in Vico's thought. Primarily it means the knowledge that is gained by mastery over the concrete situation. Thus practical knowledge must grasp the circumstances that obtain and leave aside the infinite variety that could have been. This is what Vico expressly emphasizes. Although it is true that his main concern is to show that this kind of knowledge is outside the rationalist prescription of knowledge, the point I wish to make is that this distinction refers to something deeper than the distinction between general principles and the mastery over the concrete. It establishes the idea of the consensus of the community of scholars as the source and reservoir of what we call criticism.

The very idea of comparison in literary criticism stems from Vico's concept of practical knowledge and of the community of scholars as the means of establishing validity. The canon of comparison opens up the study of works of literature from the restrictions of the singular and moves it to the broad-scale comparative historical study of literature as part of culture. The comparative idea rests on Vico's rejection of the rationalist theory of the origins of culture. The aim of this enterprise is nothing less than universal literary history as seen in the ideal history that science would establish. This.project has its beginnings, Vico insists, with the beginnings of its material, with the first recorded moment of genuine human thought and its expression of the human spirit and man's transformation of nature. It is this moment of the human spirit that the *New Science*, based on this more profound conception of poetry, makes possible for scholarship. The program Vico sets out, which would ultimately be known as comparative literary history, was breathtaking and profoundly attractive to the European literary historian, who had been obsessed with methodology. The appeal to regain the poetic consciousness of the ancient poets was the foundation of comparative historical research. In the pursuit of this ideal program it is not surprising that scholars tended to overlook or ignore the fundamental restrictions placed on the program by Vico's relational principles. By way of a conclusion I shall sum up the argument and attempt to establish the present-day common ground shared by comparative literary history and relational theory that I believe was implicit in Vico's work.

If with Vico we accept the epistemological primacy of the man-made historical world, it follows that there is no absolute to which we can appeal as the basis of the truth. It follows therefore that man is in a unique position as both the subject and the object of history. He is making his historical world as he himself is already in history and subject to historical forces that antedate him and against which he has only the recourse of self-consciousness. Therefore it is in his history-making that man encounters his own historical reality.

At the core of a possible dialogue between comparative literary history and relational theory rests the recognition that every literary historian and every literary critic must account for the fundamental non-definitiveness of the subjectivity in which his understanding moves. In other words, no one stands outside of history and no one can claim to stand free of his own experience. Texts from the past, texts from a specific tradition, are understood never in the past but in the present, in the light of the reader's experience resulting from the undeniable progress of events and subsequent texts. Similarly, the literary critic dealing with a poetic text in a comparative context of literatures and traditions knows that the poetic text will not be exhausted by his work; the object of comparative study is to establish relationships, not to reduce the text to specific circumstances, be they past or present. In both cases it is the progress of events and texts in history that brings out new aspects of meaning in the historical and critical study. Texts from the past are thus drawn into a process of understanding in the same way as are events: in the critical or scholarly encounter the text is re-actualized within a contextual framework based on the ongoing tradition to which they belong and which in some cases they have created. Our meaning cannot be separated from the text's historical process, which we have inherited in the present. Every interpretation is therefore determined by the actualization within a historical continuum.

The relational literary theorist seeks to explain why and how we arrive at shared meaning, but it is the comparatist who knows through experience that we do in fact achieve a body of knowledge that I have called the shared meaning. Every time we offer commentary on literature we participate in the tradition of commentary, which is far greater than the sum of its participants' writings, for we are fully aware that after us others will understand the same texts in a different way. And yet we are also fully aware that the texts that we study remain the same work of art, the same inexhaustible source, the fullness of whose meaning is always in process. It is a dynamic reality that is demonstrated continuously in the changing process of understanding. The form remains stable; the historicity of the text is enlarging, and the reader's understanding is always new. The principal thrust of relational literary theory today is to examine the text in all its manifestations and to oppose reductionism. From a theoretical point of view the reduction of a text to the author's intended meaning is just as inappropriate as the reduction of historical events to the intentions of the main participants. The general orientation in comparative historical study has been to establish the historical record of the development and the interrelations of literatures in the past. The distinction between relational literary theory and comparative literary history should not be blurred, for each has its perimeters of operation and these only partially coincide. But it is in this area of coincidence that I claim that the two are just as clearly indispensable to each other today as they were at the time Vico was embarking on *The New Science*.

To sum up: Vico's philosophy marked the beginning of a relational inquiry into language and thought that we can recognize today as the precursor to relational literary theory. At the same time Vico's canon of comparative analysis provided the foundation for the development of modern philology, from which comparative literary history has developed. To speak a language in Vico's terms is to have a world, to go beyond the physical limitations of the body and its needs. The successors to Vico have added, as I have tried to sketch in this chapter, that to have a world one must have an attitude or a point of view towards the world. Thus the basic philosophical problem emerges of how an individual world-view can lead to a shared view of the world. At the risk of gross oversimplification, I shall state that this problem is at the core of contemporary literary theory.

The comparative literary historian, immersed in his own historical situation, following Vico's view of philology, strives to avoid an exclusiveness of perspective. The paradoxical demand on the comparatist is to overcome the limitations of his experience of the world without leaving it or negating it. That the paradox has been temporarily resolved by so many scholars demonstrates that there is in fact a shared meaning possible. It is my contention that relational literary theory and comparative literary history consequently have today come together in mutual support.

The muddled middle of heated debate is where we often find ourselves today in the sometimes shrill and strident flurry of claims and counterclaims of theoreticians and historians, but I do *not* consider this to be a regrettable situation that affects the so-called clarity of understanding among scholars and intellectuals. Quite the contrary, I see this as a coming of age for literary studies. We are now in a position where we encompass both the practice of comparative literary history and the philosophical reflection on what it is that we do and how we do it.

PART II

Phenomenological Hermeneutics

The four chapters of this second part constitute the core argument for phenomenological hermeneutics. The four chapters correspond to the four central questions: What is a literary text? How can we say anything about the text if the text keeps changing with each reading and each reader? Is there a possibility of a shared meaning in the text, that is, an agreement about the text? And finally, what is a critical text, that is, what constitutes the critical commentary and in what way can it be distinguished from the literary text?

In responding to these questions I have attempted to give a pragmatic presentation of phenomenological hermeneutics rather than an extended historical survey, which has already been done.

A brief description of phenomenological hermeneutics, which the reader will find repeated in many places and which is correct in so far as a brief description can cope with a complex undertaking, is a starting-point: Hermeneutics is a theory of interpretation of written documents wherein the status of the interpreter is considered in the commentary. Phenomenological hermeneutics is a contemporary revision of the nineteenth-century discipline wherein the Romantic notion of establishing the author's genius has been replaced by a full consideration of the reading experience as the point of departure of the inquiry. The work of Heidegger was essential for the development of phenomenological hermeneutics, since it made possible the philosophical premise of being-in-the-world, which has proved to be the solution to the subject-object impasse. More directly involved with the contemporary merger of hermeneutics and phenomenology has been the work of Hans Georg Gadamer, *Wahrheit und Methode* (1960). Of course, the principles of phenomenological hermeneutics have been most fully elaborated in the work of Paul Ricoeur from 1970 to 1985. He began this period with numerous articles, published in various languages, but collected by J.B. Thompson under the title *Hermeneutics and the Human Sciences* (1981), which has been followed in rapid succession by the key books: *La Métaphore vive* (1975), *Interpretation Theory* (1976), *Temps et Récit* (1983), *La Configuration dans le récit de fiction* (1984), and *Le Temps raconté* (1985).

2

The Ontological Status of the Literary Text

What is a text? What is a literary text? The essential characteristics of a text are that it is written discourse with a discernible unit totality, that is, a composition, a product of a writer's labour, but I also hold that it is available only through an immersion in the text-reader relationship, which relegates the author-text relationship to the historical event of composition. If this is so, what enables us to refer to a text as literature or law, religious writing, and so on? A text belongs to a specific tradition of written discourse as long as it continues to perform the primary function of the tradition. Thus a text ceases to be a religious tract when it no longer satisfies the needs of the tradition. It may then become a historical document.

The principal function of literature is to provide the means for the redescription of the world for its readers. The capacity to bring about the configurational sense of experience and the refigurational projection of reality is the core identity of literature. Thus it is feasible that a text that was once literary can become historical or religious, as well as the inverse.

The literary dimension of a text cannot be accounted for exclusively on any of its strata, but only in its total impact on present-day readers. The strata that we shall treat in chapter 3 of the second part are the formal, historical, experiential, and hermeneutic. This functional concept of literature is derived from the phenomenological hermeneutics of Hans Georg Gadamer and Paul Ricoeur. But before engaging in the study of the text, we must be clear on what a text is.

The main concern of this chapter is the description of those characteristics of texts that enable us to grant them an identity through time, first with respect to the text as writing, then to the underlying issue of meaning, and eventually with regard to questions of reference. These issues link up at various points with other aspects of identity, such as the unity of a text, the unity of an author's work, and the unity of genre. One of my ongoing interests has been to understand how identity operates when we write literary criticism, and in this chapter I also try to address why it is that this class name is so central to our thinking and whether we can justify the concept of literature in terms of such a concept.

CRITERIA FOR IDENTITY

In recent years a number of writers have attempted to analyse textual identity in terms of the interrelations between various and successive readings of a text.[1] This kind of analysis implies that there is a conceptual connection between textual identity and the various readers' concretizations of a text, a connection that might be established by a record of a succession of readings. These conditions make up what I call the consensus criteria of textual identity. These criteria of identity have typically been regarded as essentially comprising two kinds of elements: continuity and coverage. Thus if the continuity factor encompasses the successive readings by each reader and the coverage factor accounts for the various individual readers, the combination of both factors will yield the consensus of identity. In spite of the obvious appeal of this common-sense approach to our problem, we must dismiss the consensus identity as an arbitrary construct, much like the notion of average man, that does not contribute any insight into the question of textual identity.

We must re-examine the issues and ask two fundamental questions: first, can we describe the persistence of a text as dependent on the occurrence of a succession of formal features that stand in some distinctive unity-making relationship? For example, do the opening lines of *Don Quixote* and the ensuing succession of lines that have not changed since a critical edition was established constitute the persistence of the text? The second question is: how can we account in observational terms for the way in which these formal features provide us with persistence of the entity we call *Don Quixote*? Our usual answer is clearly affirmative to the first question, but we hesitate before the second question, which demands more than an affirmative or negative answer and elicits an explanatory response. Furthermore, we may even go so far as to say that the answer to the first question is always affirmative, irrespective of whether we can successfully answer the second question. Our idea of the persistence of a text is basically a theoretical extension of our notion of the empirical persistence of ordinary objects around us. What we mean, in common-sense ordinary usage, when we speak about a literary text such as *Don Quixote* is more or less that the established sequential order of written (printed) words is the basic evidence of the entity we have designated by this title. There is no doubt whatsoever about this fact.

But the pressing objection to letting the issue rest at this point is contained in the second question I posed. How can we account in empirical terms for the way in which the persistence of the established sequence gives us a *meaningful* unit under the cover of the title? For we are not content to say that the entity *Don Quixote* is a fixed sequence of words; we press on to include the purported meaning of the full sequence, and this is where we enter the main task of my inquiry.

There is an unwarranted assumption in ordinary usage that the persistence of the sequence also carries a persistence of an established meaning of the words. It is in this light that the issue of identity is a real problem and not an intellectual game. Let us, however, suppose for the sake of argument that a *description* of a text that was not tied to an established persistence of words would be less coherent than a description given in terms of the sequence. If this were so, it would appear to follow logically that there would be a theoretical advantage in describing textual identity in terms of the established sequence. But on closer examination this argument falls short because it fails to give us any mode of linkage between formal and meaningful identity, and it is for this reason that the formal description of a text can only be the first step in the quest for textual identity. It is my contention that there is not and cannot be any intrinsic unity of meaning through time in the sense of a unity that cannot be adequately redescribed in different terms. Nor can there be any relationships that are intrinsically unity-making, in the sense of a relationship that cannot be coherently separated from its unity-making role in our search for identity. Hence the persistence of any conceivable text may be taken as a mere succession of sounds or marks only if we choose to look at it merely as sounds or marks and do not infer a unity of meaning.[2] The issue is not whether we can or cannot choose to stop our inquiry with a formal description. The real issue is whether our use of textual identity in critical discourse implies a meaningful whole, and this is an issue that clearly lies beyond the consideration of the text as the mere persistence of words in sequence.

Therefore my argument is that a text considered solely upon its formal aspects cannot have any meaning and thus can be described ahistorically as a fixed sequence. But a text with implied meaning is always immersed in the historical reality of the world of action. The specific intelligibility of writing is rooted in the pre-understanding of language as social action. Writing as communication is always historical. The writer, the medium of language, the reader, the social group that provides the means for writing, all are historical phenomena. I would therefore insist that we must constantly be reminded that symbolic mediation must be understood as social mediation.[3] If we are to understand a written page, we must first situate the page within the body of the writing, then place the writing within a particular practice of writing – newspapers, lectures, poems, and so on – and then, in the experience of social interaction, locate our page within the whole network of conventions of writing, of beliefs and commitments to these beliefs, of institutions and the whole configuration of the historical make-up of culture as we understand it. My point is a simple one and I do not want to belabour it: if we can consider the persistence of a formal sequence a first criterion of identity, the second criterion for the identification of the text is its historicity. If a text were to be deprived of its history, it would also be deprived of meaning.

There is also a third criterion of identity that I would like to propose, and this is the continuing potentiality of being read. A text of course does not achieve meaning within its own formal boundaries, but only when it passes the threshold of potentiality into the experience of a reader. The most fundamental presupposition of a literary text is that it is a mode of communication. On a written page someone has written something with a meaningful content about something for somebody else to read and therefore realize. The formal structure of a text therefore carries with it the fundamental supposition that what is written was written about something intended for someone other than the writer.[4] Thus the basic requirement of the text is a *writer*, a *referent*, and an *addressee*. The writer's use of language is covered through the consideration of the formal characteristics of the text. The historicity of writer and of the linguistic medium is considered through our second criterion. And the addressee, who in our case is the reader, becomes the basis of our third criterion. The expectation of recognition and therefore communication is a component of the writer's meaning, as Wolfgang Iser and others have so clearly shown.[5] Thus we can speak of the implied reader as part of the very process of meaning, together with form and historicity. Such is the first part of my argument, that the identity of a text is directly tied to the potential for completion of meaning as reading matter. But what is meant by reading matter, and how does the text's potential as reading affect its identity? The semantic autonomy of the text means that the author's intention and the meaning of the text no longer coincide. What the text means to its readers now matters more than what the author intended when he wrote it. If the relation of text and reader is now recognized as carrying the burden of assigning meaning, we must also hasten to add that the relation of text and reader grows out of the ability to utilize the formal patterns we have described as our first criterion, and it is also dependent on the historical encounter we have outlined as the second criterion of identity.

Nothing could be more naïve than to attempt to link meaning to an abstract, atemporal figure of reader.[6] Also let us be quick to point out that just as there is an intentional fallacy that posits author's meaning as an absolute given, there is also the fallacy of an absolute text, which raised its head with the New Criticism in North America. This is the fallacy of attempting to consider the text as an authorless entity. If the intentional fallacy is blind to the semantic autonomy of the text, the isolated-text fallacy is also blind, blind to the essential historicity of the text. The text was written by someone, about something, for someone to read. This is the basic assumption of my argument. It is impossible to cancel out the historicity of a text without reducing it to a physical phenomenon such as waves in the ocean, for even rocks have a geological history. Our question is identity, but as is now clear, the question of identity is tied to interpretation by the reader.

Let us construe this final criterion of identity as fully as possible. In spoken discourse the dialogic situation provides the full realm of identity, but a written text is addressed to unknown readers and potentially to countless readers in the future, all of whom have the capacity and the interest to read it. This universalization of the audience can lead to only one conclusion, and that is that identity can never be completely fixed; it will change, for it is the response of the present and the future, and each makes and will continue to make the text relatively important or unimportant. This potential for multiple readings is the dialectical counterpart of the semantic autonomy of the text. It therefore follows that the appropriation of the text is a process that generates the whole dynamics of interpretation and concludes with a temporary sense of identity.

My argument is that identity is an expression of understanding that depends on the interaction of three independently generated factors: the established formal sequence of written words; the history of this sequence, which includes aspects of production, value, and function as well as assigned categories of classification; and the reading experience as potential concretization. This argument is based on suppositions of a phenomenological philosophy. Of course, these views on identity of the text can be challenged. The challenge can be generated from a variety of premises. One could dispute my description of text; others can dispute that there is a valid distinction to be made for discourse as a text, and still others can argue that identity is not in any way separable from self-identity of the reader. To summarize, I have proposed three closely related criteria for textual identity. These three criteria can be regarded as providing competing accounts of textual identity, but I think of them as complementary and together constituting the essential conditions for identity. If any one of the three is missing at any time, the identity of the text in question is lacking. For example, if the sequence is altered, the necessary condition of persistence in time is denied. Secondly, if the text does not have a historical record, it has an unknown context and will necessarily be given a pseudo-historical assignation by the reader. Thirdly, if the text cannot be read, it may have existed but may have been lost, leaving only some historical traces.

The conclusion that emerges from my argument is that there is the most intimate connection between my concept of the identity of a text and my definition of a text (a spatio-temporal and qualitatively construed sequence of words with the continuous potentiality of being read). It is implicit in this concept of identity that the presence of the succession of words satisfying the three conditions constitutes at least a *prima facie* basis and perhaps even a conclusive basis for making a judgment of identity.

SOME COUNTER-ARGUMENTS

I now wish to expand my proposition that the three criteria of identity come together in an act of appropriation that bestows identity upon the text. The aim is not and can never be one of finality or an absolute truth-claim, but rather one of participation in the humanistic tradition of commentary. This affirmation will immediately bring upon me the charge of relativism from those who see the task of criticism as a quest for fixed truth. My response is that the purpose of humanistic inquiry must be above all to avoid self-deception and to enhance dialogue. [7] To my mind the highest form of self-deception is to believe that we can know the truth about ourselves by knowing a set of objective facts.

I maintain that the idea of fixed identity for a literary text is contrary to the spirit of humanistic inquiry, for if we convert the text from something discursive, something incompletely attained by continual adjustments of ideas (a process I have called appropriation) – if we do this, we turn the text into a solely physical object. Let us make no mistake about it: this hypothesis can be an escape from the responsibility for our choice among competing ideas. The urge to find the absolute is the urge to eliminate our freedom for the comfort of the mental conformist. Thus the charge of relativism against my position can be the expression of rejection of freedom and responsibility. The charge is not false; it is mistaken, because the aim of the enterprise has not been understood. The concept of identity we are proposing is not a project to get rid of the burden of thought, but quite the contrary, to join in the project of humanistic commentary. To those of us who have delved into the writings of Miguel de Unamuno there is the all too familiar claim that the thinker who sees inquiry as self-enrichment is unconcerned for his fellow man, but I argue that the opposite is the case.[8] Since literature is above all a redescription of reality, the search for fixed identity of a text would necessarily seek to reduce all possible descriptions to one and in the end deny the humanistic tradition of textual commentary.

How is it that the counter-argument is misdirected? I do not accept the either-or proposition that identity is the resulting designation of the subject-object relationship or that it is an arbitrary assignation. In the first case the identity of a text would be designated by those properties that can be recognized by the subject as the particular characteristics of a specific piece of writing. In the second case identity is designated by the maker of the text, who can be either the author or the reader. If the debate were to be limited to these two positions, I think we would be caught in a stand-off as old as the confrontation between dualistic and monistic philosophy. It is my contention that both positions lack the fundamental ground of history. The rejection of both the dualist and the monist position does not abrogate the designation of identity, but only of a *fixed* identity. My argument is that neither the reader nor the text stands alone. Both are caught up in a historical context of process and change; thus all recognition and all attribution of qualities must be temporary.

I would be remiss in not pointing out that there is an opinion of some importance that holds to the necessity of a fixed identity for the literary text. The central tenet of this position, expressed with distinction by Félix Martínez Bonati,[9] is that there is a basic stability in works of literature that serves to give a text its identity. Let me be clear why it is that I disagree with this thesis. Although the fictional character of Don Quijote, for example, has a number of features that link him to a specific socio-economic class of sixteenth-century Spain, it is not the possible verification of these indicators that gives Don Quijote his identity but rather his unique departure from the norm. My argument is that the text *Don*

Quixote is grounded in a historical context because it has formal persistence, but it is incomplete without its reader. It is the historical connection of the story in both the author's production of the text and the reader who experiences the text. When this connection is traced it may well turn out that what appears to be folly can be taken as idealism and vice versa. But my basic point is that the historical connections must not only be made with reference to the text and its historicity but also with the reader in his.

The basic disagreement with the thesis of fixed identity is that the character of Don Quijote cannot be treated as a possible-but-not-actual individual. He is neither possible nor actual. He is much more and much less, for Don Quijote has the potentiality of continuous description of shared characteristics of humanity. My response therefore is twofold. On the one hand, it is not warranted to assign a certain truth-value to the linguistic formula in words that the individual reader has not yet realized. On the other hand, there is a remarkable tradition of countless readers who have shared in the pursuit of the redescription of the world through the text, and it is in this tradition that we will find the identity of *Don Quixote*. Hermeneutics is the philosophy of self-knowledge for the writer and his readers that dismisses the epistemological folly of the quest for an established absolute truth.

The position taken by deconstructionist critics is at the other extreme of the fixed-identity thesis; their argument holds that identity is only a temporary by-product of the supplementation process.[10] This vigorous contemporary view of identity is attractive in several respects, first, because it recognizes the basic role of the reader in the process of understanding a text, and secondly because it probes deeply into the plurivocal nature of language. The fundamental difficulty I find with this position is that in rejecting the significance of the historicity of production for purposes of interpretation, deconstructionists also reject the historicity of the re-producing situation of the reader. My reasons for rejecting this position are several, and they take me into proposing what I consider to be the parallel but separate relationship of author-text and text-reader. A detour concerning some basic statements on what I understand by the term *text* is in order before we undertake the task of sketching the bifurcated status of author and reader which is essential to my concept of identity.

For purposes of clarity I would like to limit the field of inquiry: a text for our purposes is any written discourse, and a literary text is written discourse whose capacity for redescription of the world has been acknowledged. The written nature of the text is fundamental, for it effectively removes the writer from the act of realization of the text. The writer is absent from the act of reading. The relationship of writer-text is parallel but quite clearly removed from the relationship of text-reader. Five effects are immediately discernible when we pass from oral utterance to written discourse: writing fixes discourse and makes it accessible across time and space; writing also gives discourse a historical dimension and relates it to a universe of other written texts (this being the cultural phenomenon we call literature); writing makes detailed analysis possible; writing allows the receptor of the discourse to be radically distanced from the event of writing (the writer's reader becomes part of an unknown, general, and possibly alien group); the context of dialogue is replaced by a referential redescription of reality that I shall call the textual world.

Let me recapitulate my argument: a work of literature is a text of varying length, but it has an established sequence and its form is a closed totality. A work of literature is codified discourse that permits it to participate in the tradition of texts we call literature. As a work of literature a text is capable of being distinguished as a unique assemblage with its own dimensions. In other words, a literary text is an artifact that has been produced by a writer's labour as a specific work that stands alongside a vast number of others in a tradition.

The most important factor of our consideration of a text as a work of literature is the acknowledgment that it is the result of labour, that it has been produced. This concept is the basis for the *formal* stratum of the text. Since the artifact is a composition, it follows that there are discernible patterns of organization and there is an implicit structure. The philosophical foundation of all formal analysis of written discourse rests on the idea of composition. Formal inquiry of a text by its very methodological approach objectifies the discourse of a literary work and constructs a structural model; but the point I am making here is that this stratum of the text is only possible when the text is considered a product of human labour.

There is a second aspect of the text as work that I must stress before going on to the other issues of texts, and that is that a work is not only a product of labour; it is also an artifact that must be removed from the control of its producer in order to be realized. In other words, the text as work is essentially separated from its author and is inserted into the reading process at an alienating distance from its reader, a distance that is never completely overcome but that is reduced through the process that I term appropriation, following Ricoeur and Weimann. The characteristics of a text are that it is written discourse with a discernible unit totality – that is, a composition, a product of a writer's labour that is available only through an immersion in the text-reader relationship – and that the author-text relationship is the event of composition.

Following Gadamer I hold to the idea that what a text signifies does not coincide with what the author meant.[11] From the moment the text is completed and given to the reader, textual meaning and author intentions have separate and often far-removed destinies. Thus a third and also basic characteristic of a literary text is that it transcends its author's psychological and sociological conditions of production. In the words of Umberto Eco it opens to an unlimited series of readings, each of which will have a specific historicity of particular psychological and sociological dimensions. In other words, the loss of original context, which is only partial and often mitigated by historical scholarship, gives way to the necessary creation of a new context that belongs to the reader-text relationship.

The position that I take eschews the direction of Romantic hermeneutics, which sought to grasp the genius of the author as exemplified by his texts, and the contemporary path of structuralism, which would restrict criticism to reconstructing the structure of the work, or the route of post-structuralist deconstruction, which would reduce the text to the status of an event with a trace left behind. My aim is to examine the reader-text relationship and thus approach the redescribed world of the text. If we take the formal structure of the text as the *sense* of the text, then *reference* is the implicit task of redescription. Thus, with Ricoeur, let us ask what happens to discourse when we consider it in its essential constitution of human work. Since the author-reader relation cannot exist as in a dialogical situation because of the bifurcation we have described as two separate and parallel relationships, that of author-text and that of reader-text, we must examine each relationship separate from its counterpart. The reader-text relationship at first sight appears to be self-referential, with no discernible tie to the world of human action. This is a false assumption, for all literary discourse achieves meaning only by reinsertion into a historical context that is that of the reader and is certainly anchored in reality. Husserl's concept of life-world[12] and Heidegger's being-in-the-world[13] adequately describe the essence of the new context of the work. The unique referential dimension of the literary text is best explained by what Ricoeur has called the split reference of literary discourse, by which he means the interplay between the self-referential aspect of poetic language and the necessary ground in the world of human action.[14] A literary text offers its readers a purported state of affairs; this is a proposed world, which can be realized only through the intervention of the reader. The redescription of reality that ensues as the essential outcome of reading is thus the exclusive property of neither the text nor the reader but is rather the unique creation of the dynamic relationship between the two.

The final characteristic of the text is that there is a discernible mode of *taking in* the proposed world of the text by the reader. The reader as commentator has the opportunity of discovering his mode of appropriation of the text. It is not a question of imposing upon the text our finite capacity of understanding but of exposing ourselves to the text and receiving from the encounter an enriched self. Consequently the critique of ideology, a critique that is exemplified by Fredric Jameson, has a specific role in bringing about an understanding of the process of appropriation with which the reader realizes the text.

I have suggested three criteria for the identity of a literary text: continuity in time of a sequence of words (form), a historical context of production, and the possibility of realization of a text through reading. I have also engaged some of the basic positions taken on the nature of the text. There remains to consider to what extent identity of the text has an independent status from the historical context of either writer or reader, or of both. We can argue that to the extent that the unity of a text can be said to depend on formal characteristics (which can be described analytically), the unity of the text depends on the empirical fact of the writing, but as I pointed out at the start of this discussion, writing itself is meaningless if it is separated from the whole of human activity. Ultimately the identity of the text depends on how the text relates to our human interests and purposes. I do not wish to imply that I am in agreement with the thesis that a text is not fully objective matter, only that it is much more than that, which does not put in question its empirical facticity. In my tripartite description of identity I have tried to do justice to this richer notion of the text.

I turn now to my last topic: of what significance is a particular concept of identity with regard to literary criticism? I believe that it is of the greatest importance because it is usually the presupposition on which a particular system or approach of literary criticism rests for the critics who pursue that particular route. I make this judgment because I am convinced that there cannot be a general theory of literary criticism, and therefore each approach consciously or unconsciously maps out the terrain of its undertaking on the basis of what its practitioners understand the literary text to be. Before going on I would like to defend the statement that there cannot be a general theory of literary criticism. If the sole purpose of a theory is to explain, something must be explained, and this means that there must be an already existing problem or issue that calls for explanation.[15] This statement leads me to go further and argue that a theory's scope cannot be determined by its subject-matter, that is, by whatever the theory is about. The scope of the theory, if its function is to explain a pre-existent issue, is determined by its purpose and by its clarification of the problems to which it offers a solution. Further, the survival of a theory, its continued use and development, is determined by its correlation to practice.

A theory of literary criticism, if it is to be a theory at all, can only be a theory about certain features that have been selected as being the ones that matter. Thus by definition a theory of literary criticism is a specific logical argument that purports to explain the problems of dealing with a specific concept of identity of the literary text; it is not a plan to explain what literary criticism is. The purpose may be, for example, to provide the necessary rules for the solution of a certain class of problems that obtain because the text has been determined as the object of hermeneutic interpretation, or, in another case, when the text has been bifurcated into discourse and story and rules of operation are needed for the semiotic analysis of discourse. The names of the various theories of literary criticism are a capsule of identity since they allude to the basic issues that are the specific relationships that have been given a major focus as they occur in the phenomenon called the literary text. This is precisely the point at issue here. It is in the presupposition of the identity of the text that we will be able to find the essential source and direction of any approach to literary criticism. For example, a structuralist theory of criticism describes specific formal relationships as they are perceived to occur in the linguistic organization of a text. Another theory of criticism may be designed to provide the operational rules needed to examine texts as a reflection of social patterns, as is part 1, section 3, of Georg Lukacs's *Ästhetik*. Still another example would be a theory of criticism whose stipulated purpose is to provide the ground rules for establishing links between the author's insight and the text – I would cite here Carl Jung's *The Spirit in Man, Art and Literature* (New York 1966, 93). In these examples, taken at random, the theory of literary criticism can provide a solution to specific problems arising out of the work done with literary texts that have been selected as being of interest and, more importantly, that have been given a specific status of identity. In short, my claim is that the concept of identity is the benchmark of theories of interpretation.

I would now like to turn to the last of the questions I posed at the outset of this chapter. To what extent can we justify approaching literature in terms of a specific concept of identity now that we have ruled out the possibility of a general theory of literary criticism? Literary study, as I understand it, is a pluralistic encounter of individual minds. Thus we have only the choice of engaging other minds or practising advanced self-delusion and convincing ourselves that a select number of other minds see the world through our biases. I make reference to encountering other minds, and this phrase has many connotations that I endorse, but it has one that must be mitigated, for I believe that an encounter need not be synonymous with a clash; an encounter can and is often an experience of mutual enrichment. When someone asks about a specific theory of literary criticism, the very asking of the question reveals a highly developed set of commitments. Thus, if an extended discussion were to ensue on the relative validity of the theoretical proposition or propositions I hold, the exchange would only be possible in the context of a specific problem, even if that problem had not yet been clearly articulated. My argument is twofold: if there is no antecedent there can be no theoretical argument, and if the identity of the text does not emerge in the process of discussion, there is scant possibility of an understanding being reached between the discussants.

It is because I have dismissed claims to a general theory as being a reduction of reality to conform with the particular interests of the individual that we now face the root question that can be asked of all relational arguments. What can we hope to achieve through the shared experience we have been sketching as the encounter of identity-concepts? The aim of the encounter must be to formulate a framework within which alternative theories can be compared and in terms of which their features, aspects of their scope, their comprehensiveness of inquiry and adequacy of application can be ascertained.

We now come to the key question in the minds of most students of literature, which is the possibility of elaborating procedures or methods of criticism in a context I have characterized as the encounter of identity concepts. If what I have presented before is acceptable, how can we proceed so as to ensure that these observations on identity are in fact an overview of the issue and do not constitute one more theory among others? Unavoidably, there have been crucial points at which my argument has taken directions that are at least in part predetermined by my particular way of identifying the literary text. My response has two parts. First, eclecticism is not a true option, for it is no choice at all to accept diverse tenets of theories irrespective of their argument; thus, pluralism should not be taken as another name for eclecticism. And secondly, a theoretical discussion, whatever the starting point, must be able to address the issues with a degree of concomitant adequacy to the implicit or explicit concept of identity used.

Let us take the case of a historicist theory of literary criticism. Whenever we probe into the outlines of a theory, the objective of the inquiry must be to lay bare the basic premise that any historical theory would have to hold. This premise is that a historical reconstruction of the author-text relationship is a viable option to pursue, but we must also underscore that the historically reconstituted text is a particular identity-concept of the literary text and cannot be accepted as a given fact. A historical reconstruction can be aimed at and pursued with diligence, but its very premise is far more speculative than most rival theories. I would therefore turn the historical issue around. In place of arguing that the historical event of composition is the paradigm for the reconstruction of the text's meaning, I propose that the event of production, together with the formal organization, is the pre-condition for the reader's realization, which is always new.

3

Derrida and the Meaning of the Literary Text

To anyone who reflects upon the main line of contemporary academic literary criticism it is clear that its claims are impossible to verify, and paradoxical in their very formulation. The general claim to knowledge of academic criticism is that it moves the reader a step closer to the definitive meaning of the literary work. But if this were so, it follows that our age would be continuously consuming and discarding literary works of the past like so many empty containers only fit for the garbage heap of literary history. The paradox could not be greater. Academic literary criticism's aims, if realized, would destroy the very creativity it extols as literature's contribution to civilization. If critics had realized their multiple aims of exhaustive examination and description and definitive interpretation, the literary text would have become a programmed recitation of familiar tropes, sterile of any creative engagement, for the hapless reader who had been exposed to their ministrations. Of course contemporary academic criticism has failed, and the only traces that will remain for the intellectual historian to ponder are the inflated claims and talk of three generations of deluded men and women who looked for the truth through a panoply of constructs.

It is in this context that we must consider the reception of post-structuralist criticism in North America. As inflated claims gave way to the reality of the conflict of interpretations, the philosophical poverty of academic literary criticism became painfully obvious to anyone who cared to review the situation. Unreflective historicism gave way to structuralism of both French and East European varieties, but even the richness of insight of this Pandora's box of tricks could not stem the tide of scepticism and the proposition that perhaps the text is indeterminate and inexhaustible. With the publication of Paul de Man's *Blindness and Insight* in 1971 and the English translation of Jacques Derrida's *De la grammatologie* in 1976, English-speaking North Americans were suddenly faced with a philosophical radicalization of Heidegger and Nietzsche that their francophone colleagues had been debating since 1967.

I propose to proceed with my commentary on deconstruction in two parts: first the philosophical argument and the uses of deconstruction, and secondly, a critique from the perspective of phenomenological hermeneutics.[1]

According to Heidegger, Being conceals itself in the very process by which it presents itself as being. The essential case of Heideggerian philosophy is the deconstruction of the ontic mask beneath which Being makes its appearance. This is not on the stage of the world, to use a popular metaphor, but *is* the stage of the world itself. Thus Heideggerian deconstruction has as its goal the unmasking of Being. But Derrida takes the argument further. To say with Heidegger that Being is behind an ontic mask is, for Derrida, to continue the reification of Being. Derrida accepts Heidegger's account of the primacy of Being-in-the-World over all subject-object relationships that the tradition of Western philosophy has posited. Plato's Ideas, Aristotle's Forms, all constructs such as essences, categories, and so on are the various instalments in the history of philosophy, and all of these are the individual projections of the philosopher's will to power. If man is to master and possess the world, he must be able to manipulate it, and his projections are the necessary reification of Being. The Heideggerian unmasking of Being is thus the deconstruction of the subject-object relationship and therefore the rejection of the epistemological premises of the European philosophical tradition. Let us reflect for a moment on Derrida's deconstruction. It is not possible merely to remove the mask from Being; the basis of the individual projection has to be uncovered. There is no possible structure for Being that is not an individual's projection. Whereas Nietzsche replaced Being by Becoming, Derrida has gone further and replaced Becoming by the process of differentiation, which has no possible structure and is only a trace.

Two pragmatic questions assert themselves here: What is the point to deconstruction? and, How is it possible to write a deconstruction of written texts without self-destructing? I shall answer the questions from the standpoint of Derrida and his North American followers before offering my critique.

Deconstruction is the interpretative process of engaging a written text by freeing the process of *différance* from the multiple masks assumed by the structure of the text. By structure of the text let us understand the project of either author or reader. Consequently deconstruction is a liberation from all structures. Deconstruction abandons the search for knowledge since knowledge is the cover for the closure imposed by presence on the text. Now to the second question: How is it possible to write deconstruction without self-destructing? Derrida's English translator Gayatri Chakravorty Spivak provides us with a succinct answer: 'Deconstruction is a perpetually self-deconstructing movement that is inhabited by differance. No text is ever *fully* deconstructing or deconstructed. Yet the critic provisionally musters the metaphysical resources of criticism and performs what declares itself to be one (unitary) act of deconstruction' (*Of Grammatology*, lxxviii). The only conclusion we can reach is that if we accept freedom and *différance* as primary, then whatever we do must be undone; a deconstructive act does something if it simultaneously is undoing something, a mask of presences. The deconstructive interpretation is a liberating force since it destroys masks and does not replace them. What remains after the deconstructive interpretation is silence and the invitation to do it again. The text emerges emancipated from the overlayers of doctrinal interpretations. This, silence and the invitation to engage the text again in the never-ending move towards freedom, is a dialectical concept, for it both destroys and preserves. Silence is the result of the destruction of masks; the invitation to return to the text is the preservation of the possibility of engagement.

Derrida's symbol of crossing-out interpretative masks fully captures the sense of this dialectical process. He begins with the idea of fallible man and proceeds to consider each philosophy and each philosopher as a metaphysical error or dead end, but rather than propose to eliminate these errors, which would merely substitute one error for another, he states that it is the nature of human thought to construct masks in the image of each subject. There is therefore no implicit claim to progress, nor an implicit search for the correct path. The moment of understanding or insight that is gained at the expense of our predecessors gives way to our own fabrication of a new blind alley. There is an identifiable Hegelian base to Derrida's imperative that we study the works of philosophers, that is to say, that we study the errors of the past. By establishing what is implicit in a philosopher's founding concepts and in the original questions asked by the thinker, Derrida is saying we can begin a process of deconstruction. It is in the breakdown of the philosopher's system that we ourselves find the breakthrough or the insight into being.

The term *deconstruction* bears some further comment, for it is more than a description of what Derrida does in his textual commentary; it is also a procedure that operates separately from its most famous contemporary advocate. It is, in effect, an approach to textual criticism that is now used independently of what Jacques Derrida made of it. But for our purposes let it suffice to describe deconstruction in Derrida's work. Derrida's first step is to establish the boundaries of the inquiry by citing the specific text or fragment of a text on which he will focus his commentary. This initial acknowledgment is much more than an identification of the subject-matter; it is an announcement of the language that will be examined with intensity and also gives notice of the forthcoming breach of the limits of the text. For those limits signal the impasse, and it is going beyond them that brings about the insight into being. The second step is to engage in an indirect questioning of the text. This is a process of encircling, making a veritable plaything of the text's language and therefore exposing the heretofore unacknowledged suppositions and premises that serve as the ground for the text. The encirclement of the text reveals the mask of the text's language and forces into the open aspects of the necessary conditions for the statements made in the text. The commentary that ensues reveals the essential mode of thinking involved in the particular writing. In other words, the object of Derrida's commentary is not to arrive at a final answer, or even a temporary one, but rather to break down the apparent solidity of the text's argument, to demonstrate its direction and force, and to dissipate the mirage of apparent finality.

Derrida's commentary is suggestive, playful, and metaphorical, and it is only by these indirect means that he unmasks the text and exposes us to writing as experience. Written language consequently enjoys a key role in Derrida's philosophy. I can best describe Derrida's concept of language by analogy.[2] For Derrida language operates in a manner analogous to a magnetic field. The magnetic field is generated between two poles, which we can call 'the making of the text' and the text itself. In marked contrast to the suppositions of literary criticism as it has been practised in the Western world, Derrida denies that the examination of the parts can lead to the whole. In nineteenth-century philology the author and his circumstances were studied alongside the reconstruction of textual history with its variations and errors. In the twentieth century we have added the bracketed close examination of the text on its linguistic merits; we have moved into reader-reception theory, and we have even invoked the psychoanalysis of author and reader, but in all of these enterprises we have never attempted a unitary understanding of our making of texts. This state of affairs persists, Derrida asserts, because we lack philosophical freedom of inquiry, or, in his words, because we are bound up in a philosophy of presence. Derrida's position is therefore not another examination of a part of the text but a leap into the whole of it. There is, of course, a paradox involved in this concept, for, to be sure, Derrida bases his commentary on very specific written passages of the texts in question. How do we attain the whole if not through a knowledge of the parts? Derrida's mode of commentary is clear: a force-field exists and we enter into it when we begin to render the text, but our usual mistake is to pretend that we have isolated meaning and significance in the text, that is to say, that we are outside of the force-field. Derrida claims that this is the fallacy of the philosophy of presence. We are, indeed, always engaged in the force-field of absence and presence, and our rendering, as well as our commentary, can reveal our involvement in the force-field if we do not engage in conceptual isolation. Therefore, if we remain knowingly in the force-field of 'the making of the text,' we can deconstruct the gloss of Western tradition, which claims as reality what in effect is a conceptual mirage of terms we take out of texts and to which we attempt to give independent significance. Inside the rendering of the text these elements are not recognizable as parts. There is but one force-field. It is only outside the making of the text that fragments emerge and are granted quasi-permanent status by our philosophical and philological tradition. But rather than reject the tradition of textual commentary as Heidegger has done, Derrida insists that such textual commentaries are nothing less than our intellectual history. They are or have been force-fields of rendering. Each of them can be the focus of the deconstruction of the impasse of textual limitations.

There is no program here for exposing errors and correcting them. By making the text the focal point, Derrida's deconstruction is a way of revealing the composition of the text in a force-field of creative tension. This is a strategy for stripping away the varnish of self-deception in order to get to the process of rendering a text that would otherwise remain hidden. In practice deconstruction is a critique of the traditional assignation of meaning that finds its validity in the repetition of fixed concepts based on a historical archaeology of composition. In summary, therefore, we can reiterate that Derrida's use of opposition does not turn the focus around as, for example, a shift from author to reader would. The use of opposition is designed to maintain a polarity and to make visible the force-field that is language. Language is thus conceived of as the tension that comes into being with a rendering of a text in relation to writing or speaking itself. The rendering of a text is an act of writing and an act of reading, which is a form of re-writing.

Let me retrace some of the general observations I have made and call attention to the implications.

1 Writing or rendering the text is inescapably bound to the composer's linguistic instrument, and this is so not as a matter of choice or intention but rather because the medium of composition does not originate with the composer; it has and imposes historicity on the act of rendering the text. Thus the creation of a new configuration with a system of pre-existent symbols is what we do when we render a text, that is, when we write and when we read a text.

2 Derrida's philosophy of language is a dialectic that we have described through the metaphor of a magnetic field. The dialectical relationship is the central core of Derrida's philosophy. All expression, every articulation involves a negating implicit opposite to itself, because the experience – the text that the speaker, writer, or reader is striving to complete – is caught in an absence-presence polarity. Every meaning grasped in the act of composition is displacing another meaning. Thus every articulation is in process, gaining and losing its meaning in the polarity. The author's intentions can be characterized as the willed presence, but displaced linguistic elements are the absence that, together with presence, creates the polarity we have described as a force-field.

3 Derrida describes what happens when we begin to render a text. The writer or the reader makes a text. As this text is made a force-field is created by the play of differences available only in the rendering of the text. The emergent experience of rendering the text is made up of interdependent and differential impulses, which cannot possibly be assigned a fixed and established meaning. Derrida describes this instability as the power of the text, which has been turned on primarily by our ability to differentiate each element as it appears from any other that could have appeared in its place, and also by our ability to defer full significance until we have rendered more of the text and thus have enlarged the field. These two aspects of our activity of rendering a text have been joined in a singular term, *différance*. By *différance* Derrida represents what we mean in English by differentiate and differentiation as well as what we mean by deferment or to defer something.

4 The text in Derrida's philosophy is a compromised mediator for the writer or the reader; it is the threshold through which we pass into the force-field of rendering it. The writer is compromised by language, the mediating energy that makes it possible for him to enter into the force-field of writing. Similarly, the reader is compromised by the writing that gives

him his entry into reading, which as Derrida often states is but another form of writing. This fundamental dialectical concept of Derrida's was given clear articulation by Paul de Man in his essay 'Form and Intent in the American New Criticism':

Literary 'form' is the result of the dialectic interplay between the prefigurative structure of the foreknowledge and the intent at totality of the interpretative process ... The completed form never exists as a concrete aspect of the work that could coincide with a sensorial or semantic dimension of the language. It is constituted in the mind of the interpreter as the work discloses itself in response to his questioning. But this dialogue between work and interpreter is endless. The hermeneutic understanding is always by its very nature lagging behind. (*Blindness and Insight*, 31)

The form of a text emerges only as a by-product of the rendering of the text; it is not pre-established; it is a consequence of the deferment that was the making of the text by writer or reader. All meanings ascribed to a text are the necessary supplement added on in the rendering of the text by the writer or reader.

I would like to begin my response with some general remarks concerning at least part of the Derridian enterprise. There is much in the works of Jacques Derrida that I find brilliant, provocative, and highly suggestive. As I have already indicated in the expository part of this chapter, the basic revelation of the power of conceptual self-deception in all commentary on texts is a major statement of contemporary literary theory with which I concur. In fact my disagreement with Derrida's deconstruction is more a matter of emphasis than a major philosophical disagreement. I shall now concentrate on those facets of his work that I have difficulty in accepting.

Derrida's theory does not readily appear to offer the possibility of participation or even of a shared insight: 'Textuality is constituted of differences, and of differences of differences; it is by nature absolutely heterogeneous and will combine unceasingly with the forces that tend to annul it' ('La Pharmacie de Platon,' *Tel Quel* 32, p. 31). What is the result of the rendering of texts, which we do individually but also in a collective tradition? What place, if any, does literary criticism have? My answer may not be satisfying to most deconstructionist critics, for it appears to me that Derrida is saying that the rendering of texts, the writing of commentary, is only an articulation of a kind of free-play. Because one cannot determine the centre of meaning and thus exhaust the totality, one can only aim at becoming a better and more adept player; for in each rendering when we give a temporary centre to a text – as we must in order to write or to read – we are in fact adding a supplement to the text and this necessary supplement is temporary; it is floating and transitory as a construct, and it serves but it cannot survive as a significant statement about the text; it is always a supplement, which has been the necessary by-product of playing the game.

Derrida's rejection of structuralism is based on his view that the separation of the signified from the signifier is impossible. In ordinary language, Derrida does not accept the concept that one can separate thought and words. If one accepts the separation of the signified and the signifier, Derrida holds, by extension one would also have to accept the concept of private language, the idea that univocal substances exist and that a pure present exists. Derrida rejects the theory of knowledge that holds that there is such a thing as knowledge that one can acquire and hold as so much capital accumulation. All of these ideas, including structuralism, come from a metaphysical premise of absolute presence, which has led thinkers to believe that in spite of their own finite limitations there exists an absolute fullness of knowledge that is the ideal goal for all inquiry.

The initial problem for Derrida is how he can write and speak without finding himself inextricably involved in the language of presence that makes up our Western tradition. This appears to be a perfect philosophical paradox, for the very denunciation of the metaphysics of presence is accomplished with words that are no sooner used than they themselves take on all the implications of a confident progression towards the absolute truth, that is, the very illusion they have denounced. I state this now in order to introduce some commentary on Derrida's own language. Derrida, like Heidegger before him, attempts to use language in such a way that it remains open and does not fall into an illusory construction of nouns and verbs building up to the mirage of substance.

Language is bound by an essential temporality; it is, in Humboldt's terms, energy and can never be fixed into presence without its being altered. Even as we become aware of the sense of language, it has already moved beyond us, so that at the very moment of presence it is already absent. The form that sense takes in our reading is what Derrida calls *trace*. The essential point to be made here is that all language is available only as a trace. This is to say that, in order for us to be aware of meaning, it must already have happened. The Hegelian dictum quoted by Jameson to describe the Derridian formula is worth repeating: 'Essence is what has already taken place.'

Derrida rejects the view that meaning is the grasping of some feature of a stable configuration of the world. What we call meaning is in fact a nostalgia for the past. No sooner have we claimed to have the meaning of a text than we are already into what *was* and not what *is*, because we have closed the search for meaning. Alternatively, Derrida considers meaning not as that which was but as that which is; this is the idea of meaning as a dynamic will to know that fuels the deferral of closure. This view holds that the meaning of a written text is always deferred in the process of an endless series of re-interpretations in which no concept can be considered self-evident or self-sufficient since the interpreter is caught up in the process himself. The most significant consequence of this idea is that it removes from sign the possibility of limitation to fixed characteristics of a stable configuration, since meaning exists in deferral rather than in nostalgia. The sign is at once opaque and transparent since it can be referred towards materiality and it can refer conceptually towards itself.

Because of the nature of Derrida's concept of meaning there looms a logical trap in the deconstructionist project, one into which most deconstructionists fall save Derrida himself and perhaps the proto-deconstructionist C.S. Peirce. Deconstructionist critics are caught up in the very textual logic they try to deconstruct, which forces them into the alternatives of unrestricted play or nostalgia for the past. There seems to be no way out if Derrida's idea of meaning is taken out of context.

The way to overcome this trap is to be found in the recognition that the very process of deferral constitutes a tradition. But this awareness has yet to be articulated by deconstructionist critics and is present only by implication in Derrida's writing, in his tacit acknowledgment of the philosophical texts on which he comments – that is, Plato, Rousseau, Descartes, Husserl – as part of the tradition of Western philosophy.

Turning to some of the practical implications of Derrida's theory, first, there is always an irremovable gap between a text and its meaning, and it follows that all interpretation is generated in an effort to fill the gap or, in his words, to fill the essential absence in the text itself. A second implication is that a text can never have or be given an ultimate meaning. A third corollary is that all interpretations of a text are superimposed; the text is like a massive onion that we can never finish peeling. There are layers upon layers of the signified, each of which in its turn becomes a signifier and thereupon gives rise to another layer of signified. This is the very stuff of which the intellectual history of Western man is made.

On several occasions, for want of a better term I have referred to Derrida's writings as constituting a philosophy, and indeed some critics in North America have attempted to make his thought operate as a system.

There is, however, a profound repudiation of system at the very core of Derrida's writing. Because Derrida rejects any concept that claims to describe the fundamental content of reality, his own critique, if it is transformed into a system, falls into self-contradiction and self-elimination. It is for this reason, I believe, that he has maintained throughout that his deconstruction cannot be turned into a reverse construction.

There is another logical problem in Derrida's writing to which I would like to call attention. If we eliminate the separation between signifier and signified as Derrida has insisted we do, then ought we not also to abandon the words *signifier* and *signified* themselves. Derrida does not suggest that we should or could remove the words from our conceptual framework, and indeed makes extensive use of the two himself. The argument Derrida gives is brilliant but, I believe, incomplete. He argues that sign is itself determined by the opposition of signified. In other words, the two must appear together and the false implication arises when one engages one separate from the other. I quote from *L'Ecriture et la Différence*: 'We cannot do without the concept of sign, we cannot renounce the metaphysical complicity involved in it without at the same moment renouncing the very work of criticism which we are directing against it, without running the risk of erasing the difference in the inner identity of a signified which has absorbed its signifier into itself, or, what amounts to the same thing, has completely exteriorized it' (*Writing and Difference*, 412–13). The most important reason why we cannot eliminate systems of distinctions such as signified and signifier is that we must use models to cope with reality. As long as the models are understood to be heuristic devices and not reality itself, we have not fallen into the conceptual trap of absolute presence.

I agree with Derrida's argument and by analogy now use it to oppose his view of literary criticism. I do not accept Derrida's view that literary criticism must inevitably end up wholly involved with itself as a hydra biting its own tail. The subtle but powerful concept of the critical method as a heuristic device that produces a play on the original text, a play on the text that is worthy of sharing, is the hermeneutic position that I support. It is, to use Hillis Miller's metaphor, both the host and the parasite, for the critical commentary both provides food for the text's realization and becomes food for its readers, who form a communion, and is further derivative and dependent on the literary text.

Post-structuralist deconstructionists have ignored the fundamental issue regarding the origin and substance of all natural languages as social action. It is this blindness that has led them to deny the validity of participation in a community of shared commentaries. This concept of a community with a clear sense of past significance in present meaning through a tradition of commentary is at the very core of phenomenological hermeneutics. From Gadamer's elaboration of tradition in *Truth and Method* to Ricoeur's insistence on social action as the ground of language, we have had a series of theoretical clarifications of the nature of understanding as a human achievement mediated by the explanatory procedures used by the commentators, procedures that precede interpretation and accompany it in its transmission. Therefore the principal objection to post-structuralist deconstruction raised by phenomenological hermeneutics is the collective reality of commentary.

While the deconstructive critic's task is to identify the implicit deconstruction that is already in the text and to refrain from imposing closure on the text – that is, from assigning a specific meaning to the text, which is the inevitable experiential task of the reader – phenomenological hermeneutics adds a fourth dimension, which is the knowing participation in the tradition of the quest for self-knowledge.

The logic of deconstruction criticism is to put into question any statement that might appear to be a positive conclusion, and therefore deconstructive critics try to make their own stopping points distinctively divided, paradoxical, arbitrary, or merely indeterminate. That is to say, these stopping-points are not the pay-off, though they may be emphasized by a summary exposition, whose logic leads one to reconstruct a reading in view of its end. The achievement of deconstructive criticism lies in the delineation of the logic of texts rather than in the posture with which or in which critical essays conclude. The goal is not to reveal the meaning of a particular work but to explore the forces and structures that recur in reading and writing. The challenge and subsequent rejection of historicist criticism has been devastating because deconstruction criticism has taken pains to point out the self-deception of the critic who fixes the referential aspect of poetry with regard to his own particular imagination and who purports to have found a universal truth of meaning. Phenomenological hermeneutics agrees with this critique of historicist criticism, but we in turn object to the premature terminus to the discussion that is imposed by deconstruction.

Deconstruction appeals to many in North America because of the negative truth it fosters – that is, because it exposes false pretences on the part of critics – but it has also been open to the charge of nihilism because it postulates the all-encompassing rejection of all other interpretations as being nothing more than supplementary figural superpositions assigned to the text by the critic in order to make the text over and make it conform to his own particular spectrum of values. If we set aside the claims and counter-claims of post-structuralism as it is known today and assess the writing of the major deconstructive critics like the late Paul de Man and his Yale colleagues J. Hillis Miller, Geoffrey Hartman, and Harold Bloom, as well as other notable critics like Sam Weber, Barbara Johnson, and Robert Young, we will have a clearer contrast between the position held by this movement and that espoused by phenomenological hermeneutics.

The various critical deconstructions of target texts produce lucid narrations that in turn bring to the surface of the reader's experience ambiguities and ambivalence more profound and disturbing than anything the figural text had heretofore engendered. The reason for this reversal is clear: while the direction of historicist criticism is relentlessly towards the reduction of the text to a single preferred interpretation, the direction of deconstruction is to open the text up so radically that no single interpretation can ever suffice. Deconstruction thus treats each previous critical interpretation and its truth-claims not as external accidents or deviations to be rejected but rather as manifestations or displacements of forces emanating from the work itself. Consequently, deconstruction does not dispense with the referential aspect of literary language; what its adherents do hold is that reference is essentially indeterminate.

The crucial question still remains unanswered: for whom do the deconstructionist critics write and for what purpose? We will rule out self-indulgence and self-promotion and press the question again. The answer is clear: they write for an internationally constituted group of persons concerned with common issues of language, philosophy, and literature. But do they write to convince, to win over other points of view, to respond to other views, and so forth? Let us say that they write primarily to participate, whatever other motives may obtain in individual cases. This conclusion is one that remains unexamined by post-structural deconstructionist critics, and it is the essential question to which phenomenological hermeneutics responds.

I have characterized literary criticism as a form of celebration within a community; this is an international community of individuals who participate in the tradition of textual commentary. In order to participate, one must first recognize the community, and in order to engage in the multi-voiced conversation one must recognize the validity of other voices. If we are to engage in conversation, we must be willing to listen as well as to speak, and this means that we must be able to accept critical commentators as generators of new descriptions rather than as authors of statements moving closer to or further from the truth.

Of course, there can be no celebration in a community at war with itself. A common ground must be established, and this is precisely the failure of post-structuralist deconstruction and the aim of phenomenological hermeneutics. Let us return to this concept of community. It is not a utopia I am writing about, but rather of the most powerful force in intellectual life, one with which we are all familiar, although few openly acknowledge it, and this is the insatiable need to engage in dialogue and gain for ourselves the wisdom of personal insight. I have spoken before colleagues in many cities throughout the world, some far removed from my own culture and of whose sensibilities I am partially ignorant, but a bond has prevailed that is far stronger than all the obvious differences. This bond is the recognition that we are members of a community whose main purpose for being has been and is ever to enlarge the dialogue into an oratorio of past significance in present meaning.

Phenomenological hermeneutics is not another way of knowing that can be assigned its role by deconstructionist critics. It is more accurate to characterize it as another way of coping with reality, and one that includes post-structuralist scepticism. Therefore there is one fundamental point of disagreement between phenomenological hermeneutics and the post-structuralist deconstruction of Jacques Derrida and his North American colleagues. They do not recognize the essential reality of literary criticism as a shared experience. On the contrary, phenomenological hermeneutics has postulated its domain as the world of social action and the concept of community. A community is defined by a shared activity. It is the engagement in social action marked by a feeling of a unity but also an activity wherein individual participation is completely willing and not forced or coerced. In short, for there to be a community there must be a consciousness of the collective identity and there must also exist a strong sense of purposive sharing among its members.

4

Ricoeur and Shared Meaning of Interpretation

'The principal value in reading great works of literature lies in what they can help us to become.' This is an age-old maxim heeded by countless generations and repeated as an article of faith from Plato's *Symposium* to the appreciations of the classics by George Santayana. But many of my generation who have lived through the horrors of the Second World War and who have witnessed the magnitude of man's crimes against humanity have come to dismiss our tradition of humanistic learning as the inconsequential ornamentation of the leisure class. After all, it is argued, some of the most vicious violations of human dignity were perpetrated by men who read the classics, who loved music and art and were conversant with the writings of the great philosophers. I wish to offer a counter-argument in support of the humanities.

The writings we consider the classics of our tradition, the works of Aristotle, Lucretius, Dante, Shakespeare, Cervantes, Milton, Goethe, Shelley, Keats, Galdós, Rilke, Proust, Joyce, Borges, to name a few of our acknowledged masterpieces, *if* considered as feats of genius performed by their authors, would merely be temporally marked events of human accomplishment, and if they had perished before our day, as so many ancient texts have, they would not have forfeited any of their truth or greatness as events, but they would have become inconsequential to us. We can neither take away nor add to their past value or inherent dignity. It is only they, these written texts, that can add to the present value and dignity of our minds – but, and this is the thesis I will defend, not because they can teach us anything about our world, not because they are to be emulated in style or design, not because we are exhorted to follow some lofty idealism through the reception of the accumulated wisdom of the past – none of these will suffice. The reading of great works of literature contributes to the making of our world in so far as they oblige us to remake our world-view through their power of redescription and force us to take a stand in our response to their truth-claims. This is the general response I give to the central question of literary theory, what is literature? My argument develops a relational theory of literature and rejects the validity of all claims to definitive interpretations.

I have consistently argued that a general theory of literary criticism is a contradiction in terms since a theory by definition is an explanation of some perceived problem or set of problems. The explanation must follow the recognition and designation of the problem. The problem we confront here is that of the purported definitive interpretation of poetry. Is there an interpretation of a text that is so certain that no reasonable person could question it? My response is no. Further, I think that the pursuit of definitive interpretation is futile and misguided idealism. I shall argue here for critical interpretation of texts that is free from the notion that critical commentary must centre around the discovery of a permanent interpretation. In particular I believe it is imperative that critical commentary be freed from the notion that its function is to explain what is not clear about the text to ordinary readers.[1] My theoretical position is best identified as phenomenological hermeneutics. I shall proceed in three stages: first, I shall make a brief statement of operating principles, drawing distinctions between my position and that of Romantic hermeneutics in the past and post-structural theory in the present; secondly, I shall discuss the idea of the text; and, finally, I shall outline the consequences of phenomenological hermeneutics for textual study.

Since 1960 the position we now identify as phenomenological hermeneutics has been developing as a consequence of the writings of Hans Georg Gadamer, especially his *Truth and Method* (1960), the later writings of Martin Heidegger, and primarily the work of Paul Ricoeur, notably *The Rule of Metaphor* (1976), *Interpretation Theory* (1976), *Hermeneutics and the Human Sciences* (1981), and more recently *Time and Narrative* (1984).

By way of introduction to philosophical hermeneutics in general and phenomenological hermeneutics in particular I would like to provide a guide through the labyrinth of contemporary, literary theory. Let us consider two basic focal points of theoretical concern; one, which we will call explanation, is an intentional strategy dependent on deductive or inductive reasoning to present some issue to another person; the other is understanding, a temporary conclusion in a process of inquiry.[2] Now, by sketching the relationship between the two points I will outline in a rough but I hope effective way the most salient characteristics of four major contemporary theoretical clusters: historicist theories, which are sometimes linked with the Romantic hermeneutics of Schleiermacher; formalist theories; philosophical hermeneutics; and post-structuralist theory, also called deconstruction.

Historicist theories are based on an explanation of the text in terms of its context at the time of composition, with the aim of gaining a definitive understanding of the text. Thus diagrammatically we could show this cluster as an arrow going from explanation to understanding. Formalist theories, on the other hand, presuppose an understanding of the text and aim at a full and definitive explanation. Clearly these two clusters of theory are not incompatible, but they do operate on quite different premises and accept very different forms of evidence. Formalist theories in a diagrammatic rendering would show an arrow going from understanding to explanation. Philosophical hermeneutics differs from the previously discussed theoretical clusters in that the relationship between explanation and understanding is held to be a reciprocal movement, that is, a dialectical process of tension and interaction. A diagram would illustrate this cluster with a double-headed arrow signifying the reciprocal process.

Deconstruction is a contemporary form of radical scepticism where there is no movement between explanation and understanding. Explanation turns back on itself as another text derived from an earlier one, and understanding becomes a mode of supplementation that is only sufficient to its own ends of playing the game. The distinction between explanation and understanding is thus rejected, since a purported explanation of a text would only be a secondary phase of purported understanding. In our diagram each focal point would be represented by an arrow turned in on itself.

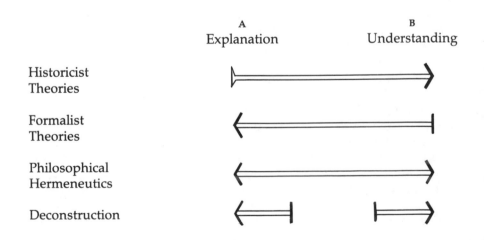

Each of the four clusters of theories operates within its own perimeters of inquiry, and each must establish its rules of operation within its domain. This does not mean that one can agree with all four premises, for that would lead to an empty eclecticism. Indeed, as I shall attempt to demonstrate, there is an argument that in my view makes philosophical hermeneutics a more satisfying basis for literary criticism.

The dialectic of philosophical hermeneutics is the core that holds together the cluster of theories by such varied thinkers as Gadamer, Habermas, and Ricoeur. The dialectic between explanation and understanding has three general propositions. The first is that it is impossible to know anything where there was not a presupposition to the inquiry. Pre-existing systems of inquiry are thus always inherently part of the way we conceive our purposes and choose the means to realize them. A second general proposition common to philosophical hermeneutics is an anti-idealist position, which reworks the dialectical logic of Hegel but rejects his conclusion of an absolute. This means that philosophical hermeneutics accepts the irreducible contingency of both the thinker's own strategies and of reality itself. The truth that emerges from these theories is the truth of self-knowledge.

The third general proposition is that there is an intentional structure in both explanation and understanding. Not only is there intentionality behind explanation in the very choice of subject and in the way in which the thinker addresses his object of inquiry, but there is also an intentional framework in the social conditions of the thinker that affects his understanding. Further, both intentional structures are dialectically related. There are no absolutes; there is no definitive truth; but there are means of reflecting on how it is that the thinker knows what he thinks he knows.

I would now like to turn to phenomenological hermeneutics and comment on the principles of inquiry that are derived from Heidegger, Gadamer, and Ricoeur and that constitute a theory of literature. If we accept that hermeneutics is a reflective theory of interpretation, then phenomenological hermeneutics is a reflective theory of interpretation grounded in the presuppositions of phenomenological philosophy. The basis of a phenomenological hermeneutics is derived from questioning the subject-object relation, and it is from this questioning that we first observe that the idea of objectivity presupposes a relationship that encompasses the allegedly isolated object. This encompassing relationship is prior to and more basic than any categories we may wish to construct. The term used by Heidegger to designate this fundamental relationship is *being-in-the-world* (*Being and Time*, 78–90).

The Heideggerian term expresses the primacy of belonging, of partaking of the world, which precedes reflection. This term and others similar to it in the work of Gadamer and later phenomenological philosophers all attest to the priority of the ontological category of *Dasein*, which we are, over the epistemological and psychological category of the subject that reflects on itself. Thus it is that we can say with Ricoeur that 'the most fundamental phenomenological presupposition of a philosophy of interpretation is that every question concerning any sort of being is a question about the meaning of that being' (*Hermeneutics and the Human Sciences*, 114).

OPERATING PRINCIPLES

The first principle of phenomenological hermeneutics is that every question we ask concerning the text to be interpreted is a question about the meaning of the text. The meaning of a text is to be derived from an inquiry into the make-up of a text, which is form, history, the reading experience, and the interpreter's self-reflection.

The second principle of a phenomenological hermeneutics is that the traditional model of textual communication, which moves from writer to text to reader, is here supplanted by a bifurcated model that construes two separate and parallel relationships: first, in temporal priority, the writer-text relationship, and secondly, the text-reader relationship. The term *author* is reserved as a value-concept of the historical context.

The writer-text relationship is akin to the creative process in any human endeavour by which man's labour individuates his work as a unique statement of self. But once the work is given over to the readers, this relationship has ended; there is no retroactive control over the created work, just as in the case of natural children, they are individuals who will find their own way. The psychological intentions of the writer or parent are of no consequence except to him. Textual intentionality must unfold before the reader as part of the reader's experience.

If the reader is to grasp the meaning of a literary text, he must be able to recognize its singularity as the composition of an author. This event of grasping the style of the literary work of art is not to be sought in the historicity of the author but rather in the very form of the text. This aspect must be further developed if the role of the author is not to be a source of confusion and misunderstanding. Since style is labour that individuates, whether it be that of the artisan making a cabinet or an author writing, it is the sign of composition of structuration that produces an individual work, and therefore it retroactively designates its author. Thus it is that the distinctive individuating features of a producer are an essential part of stylistics in literary criticism, and the term *author* is a value-concept in literary history. The singular configuration of the literary work of art and the singular configuration of the author are strictly correlative. Unamuno understood the nature of writing and the writer when he argued that man individuates himself in producing individual works. The signature of the author is the mark of this relationship.

The essential characteristic of a literary work is that it transcends the psychological and sociological conditions of its production and thereby comes into a new relationship that cannot be circumscribed. This new relationship is an unlimited series of readings each of which is itself situated in its own sociological, psychological, and cultural context. Thus the third principle of phenomenological hermeneutics is the recognition that the text is cut off from its original context and is thrust into an alien context through the act of reading.

It must be emphasized once again that there is no longer a situation common to the writer and the reader. If we have rejected the search for the psychological intentions of another person – the author – which were supposedly concealed behind the text, and if we do not want to reduce interpretation to the post-structuralist free-play, then what remains as our domain of inquiry? My position is that the task of interpretation is to explicate the type of being-in-the-world that is unfolded in and through the text.

Following Hans Georg Gadamer's philosophy, we concur that the human condition is understood essentially as a dialogue of realization for the person belonging to and interacting with a tradition in a community of commentary. The fourth principle of phenomenological hermeneutics derives in part from *Truth and Method*; it is the idea that the hermeneutic encounter is one of overcoming the initial alienating strangeness of the text for the reader. The metaphor of distance serves to describe this encounter and the ensuing process of continuing tension. In other words, there is an initial antinomy between text and reader, an opposition between the alienating distanciation and the thrust towards appropriation by the reader. I hasten to add that this is not an either-or proposition but rather a process that is rooted in the problematic of the literary text. To put it in Ricoeur's words: 'In my view, the text is much more than a particular case of intersubjective communication, it is the paradigm of distanciation in communication. As such, it displays a fundamental characteristic of the very historicity of human experience; namely that it is communication in and through distance' (*Hermeneutics and the Human Sciences*, 131).

The fifth principle of the hermeneutics I am proposing describes the central process of appropriation of the text in the reading experience. Appropriation is the English translation for the German *Aneignung* used first by Ricoeur in 1972 and more recently by Robert Weimann. The term means to make one's own what was initially alien. As I have stated above, the task of phenomenological hermeneutics is to overcome the cultural distance and historical alienation of the text. The goal of appropriation is realized only in so far as the meaning of the text is actualized for the present reader. Appropriation therefore is the process of actualization of meaning in a text addressed to a reader. It is consequently a dialectical concept of dynamic process whose result is an event of taking over what was initially the thought of others. The reading experience as an event in present time set in the midst of the historicity of the reader is the new event that replaces the writer's event.

If we begin the task of interpretation with the understanding that the literary text has an autonomous status with regard to the author, we have three clear options for the study of the text: we can explain the text in terms of its internal relations, its structure; we can respond to the text, read it, and comment on it; and we can attempt to relate these two, that is, the formal explanation with regard to the understanding of the reading experience. This latter course of action is that of phenomenological hermeneutics, and in order to attain it we must encounter the text as form, but also as a historical, distant event, and finally as a historically present event. Consequently, our sixth principle is that the starting point is the formal organization that is subsequently tied to the traces of its historical origins, but it is clearly and openly reconstituted as a contemporary event for the reader, who is the necessary agent of meaningfulness. The reader function becomes the assimilating concretizer created by the experience of reading the poem and thereby participating in the poetic world of the text.

The seventh principle of the hermeneutics I am sketching will be a clarification of what it can attain and what it cannot. Phenomenological hermeneutics differs from Romantic hermeneutics in at least one essential proposition: whereas nineteenth-century hermeneutics sought to link the content of literary texts to the psychological disposition of the author or to the social conditions of the community in which the texts were produced, phenomenological hermeneutics is ultimately directed to the examination of the text as a reconstituted reality that takes in historical considerations but is grounded in the phenomenon of the reader's appropriation. We must also take care to distinguish our enterprise from any literary or textual criticism of an anti-historical character, such as structuralism or post-structuralism. The seventh principle is the recognition that the establishment of fixed meaning is impossible and that the conflict of interpretations is inescapable, but rather than evade this fact we seek participation in the tradition of humanistic commentary, which Paul Ricoeur has called the hermeneutics of the textual refiguration and configuration of world.

These principles of phenomenological hermeneutics that I have outlined constitute a literary theory and set out a way for literary criticism to follow. In summary, these are:

1 Every question we ask concerning the text is a question about meaning.
2 There are two separate and parallel relationships: author-text and text-reader.
3 Text transcends the conditions of production and comes into a new relationship that cannot be circumscribed.
4 Hermeneutic encounter is one of overcoming the initial alienating distance of the text for the reader.
5 Appropriation is the process of actualization of meaning in a text addressed to a reader.
6 The starting point of criticism is the study of the formal organization of the text.
7 The establishment of fixed meaning is impossible since the text is inexhaustible.

I would like to return to the central concept of the literary text in order to comment subsequently and briefly on the consequences of this theory for literary criticism.

THE FOUR DIMENSIONS OF THE LITERARY TEXT

The fourth and final dimension of the literary text is the hermeneutic level, which is self-understanding on the part of the commentator. The first three dimensions, it will be recalled, are the formal or semiotic, the historical, and the phenomenological, that is, the reading experience. The idea that links phenomenological hermeneutics to hermeneutics in general is the premise that the literary text is the medium through which the reader-commentator-critic understands himself. This idea is grounded in Gadamer's insistence on the subjectivity of the reader. The text, as we have said, is appropriated by the reader, who, in so doing, applies it to his present situation. But it must be underscored that the initial distance of the text is not abolished by appropriation; it is basically transformed from an alienating situation to one of understanding without the illusions of romanticism. Appropriation is thus an understanding of distance. Further, and of essential importance, we must recall that appropriation is mediated by the structural objectification of the text, since appropriation does not respond to the illusory author or his intentions; it responds to the explanation of the text as described through formal analysis. Once again Paul Ricoeur sums up our position: 'Perhaps it is at this level of self-understanding that the mediation effected by the text can be best understood. In contrast to the tradition of *cogito* and to the pretension of the subject to know itself by immediate intuition, it must be said that we understand ourselves only by the long detour of the signs of humanity deposited in cultural works. What would we know of love and hate, of moral feelings and, in general, of all that we call the *self*, if these had not been brought to language and articulated by literature? Thus what seems most contrary to subjectivity and what structural analysis discloses as the texture of the text, is the very medium within which we can understand ourselves' (*Hermeneutics and the Human Sciences*, 143).

It is this return to the consideration of the consequences of interpretation that most clearly distinguishes the phenomenological hermeneutics of Paul Ricoeur from any of the various interpretative schools that have derived from Heidegger. Ricoeur's insistence on interpretation as a redescription of the world and his dismissal of the critic's implicit claim to unveil the text as a mirror of the world has forced literary critics to take a stand on their refiguration of the world without the shield of purported objectivity or the ideal concept of author's intentions.

Let us be clear on this matter of consequences. Ricoeur does not propose that reading great works of literature will produce great men. But quite directly what Ricoeur does hold is that reading of literature engages us in the activity of refiguration of the world, and as a consequence of this activity the moral, philosophical, and aesthetic questions of the world of action become our questions, to which we must respond.

The long detour of the consideration of the humanities as they are inherited by us in literature, history, and philosophy is a necessary trip according to Ricoeur because it is only amidst the engagement with our cultural heritage that we can find the freedom to redescribe the world in our own experience of self in the world of action. The function of literary criticism based on phenomenological hermeneutics is to move from the consideration of the text first as form, then as history, on to experience, and finally to self-understanding.

THE CONSEQUENCES FOR LITERARY CRITICISM

We now move from literary theory to literary criticism, and the first step is to indicate what the goal of criticism is to be. In a word, the aim of a mode of literary criticism that is unencumbered with false premises is the elucidation of the critic and his readers.[3] Elucidation is accomplished by the critic and his readers when they put into play the knowing appropriation of the literary work. Putting into play is a key concept that Ricoeur has taken from Gadamer, and we should take care to define it.

The activity of putting a text into play is not determined exclusively by the consciousness that plays, that is, the reader. The players are participants, for the activity itself has its own way of being. Putting a text into play is an experience that transforms those who participate in it – the critic and his readers. The subject of the aesthetic experience is not the critic himself but rather what takes place in the activity. We often say that we play with an idea; what we mean by this common expression is that we take up an idea and engage it: there is an essential give and take, a to-and-fro movement in this activity. We also say that an idea is played out, or that a part is played, or that something is in play between one place and another. All these expressions of ordinary language reveal that putting into play is something other than the exclusive mental activity of a subject. The *in-itself* of putting into play is such that even in a solitary situation there must be something with which one plays.

Whoever is engaged in putting into play is also played himself, for the rules of the game impose themselves upon the player, prescribing the to and fro and delimiting the field where the activity takes place. Now, the essential point to make here is that there is a strict relation between putting into play and the presentation of a world, and this relation is absolutely reciprocal. Since the definition of literature we hold is that of a tradition of texts with a maximum capacity for the redescription of the world, it follows that the game we play as readers of and commentators on literature is that of world-making.[4] As a corollary of the proposition we also hold that the literary dimension of texts, their literariness, is precisely their propensity for putting into play the heuristic fiction of the world.

The literary critic of the past well understood that art only abolished the non-metamorphosed aspects of reality. In this sense the task of the critic has always been one of recognition rather than cognition. The problem has been that this activity has been caught in a trap between the reflective Kantian tradition and speculative Hegelian tradition of philosophy. However, the proper place of criticism is not in either camp, but rather at equal distance from both traditions, accepting as much from one as from the other but opposing each with equal vigour. Consider, for example, how it is that in a theatrical representation the critic recognizes the character and the roles that are being played and responds to them with the immediacy of the representation on stage. Drama critics of the sensibility of the late Clifford Leech clearly recognized the paradox of their critical activity.[5] This most imaginary of human creations, the representation of life *as if*, demands our recognition before we can perceive originality. As that which is recognized, the presented being is what is retained in its essence; it is stripped of all that is accidental and happenstance. A representation of *Hamlet* demands our recognition before we can appreciate the fullness of its immediacy. There is therefore an essential link between the fictional fact, its capacity for figuration, and the critic's task of recognition of the essential dimension of the fiction.

The four dimensions of the literary text that I have outlined in the preceding sections can be recast as stages of operation for literary criticism. Let us examine them as a sketch of a mode of practical criticism. The formal dimension of the text is the system of signs, their rules of operation, and their interrelationships. This level of inquiry is one of semiotic analysis of the linguistic and structural features that every text has as composition. At this level we respond to the general question, How does the text operate?

The second dimension of the text is the historical. This level of inquiry stems from the basic presupposition that all texts and all readers are historical and that the historical dimension is always a factor of some consequence. The historicity of the text has an implicit tension with the historicity of the reader. As discourse it is written language addressed to someone about something. Thus, in its split reference between internal and external references there is the undeniable dialectic of the historical ground of the text and the distinct ground of the reader. At this level we operate on semantic inquiry as we seek to bring the dialectic of past significance and present meaning into focus. The general question we respond to at this stage is, What does the text speak about?

The third dimension of the text is the phenomenological level of the reading experience. At this level we turn to the consideration of experiential aspects of the text-reader relationship as we examine the textual strategies and the reader's modes of reception. Obviously, this stage of our study of the text coincides with the reader-reception theory of our colleagues from Constance.[6] This third dimension of the text therefore yields critical commentary, which we can identify as the essence of the reading experience. It should be stated once again for clarity that phenomenological reader-reception theory is not concerned with the individual experience of reading but only with the essence of such an experience. The general question we pursue at this level is, What does the text say to me that is common to the reading experience of others?

The fourth and final dimension of the text is the hermeneutic level of self-knowledge. At this level we encounter the undercurrent of tension between the text's autonomy and the assimilating force of the reader's appropriation. At this level there is a reflective assessment of what Gadamer has called the fusion of horizons; it is this act of dialogic unity with the text that is the very core of what is called the hermeneutical experience. The question here is, How have I read the text?

The critical commentary on a literary text must move progressively through the four stages I have sketched here, and any contribution that is to be made towards the elucidation of the critic's readers will result from the conjunction of the four stages. But let us not make the mistake of treating this approach as if it were a method for the determination of the definitive meaning of the text. The essential aim of this mode of literary criticism is not to establish any mirage of objective truth about the text, but rather to elucidate the shared experience of reading the text with the essential claim of the stock-taking fourth dimension of the text being that the only form of truth we encounter is the truth of self-knowledge. The questions we ask constitute the dialogic experience of the reader-text relationship, and the structured questions we propose as a basis for literary criticism:

1 How does the text operate?
2 What does the text speak about?
3 What does the text say to me?
4 How have I read the text?

These questions constitute a mode of critical performance that is designed to participate in the community of commentary rather than indulge in the fantasy of objective and definitive interpretation. I shall demonstrate this approach to literary criticism in the third part of this book.

The primary task of a literary critic's work therefore is to participate in and contribute to the tradition of commentary we have inherited from the humanists. In this light I consider Giambattista Vico to be the founder of modern relational literary criticism. One of the constant objections that are made to any literary theory that holds the literary text to be indeterminate and the work of art to be inexhaustible is the charge of inconsequential commentary, which comes about mainly because of the claim that the truth is unattainable and one reading experience is purportedly as good as any other. This objection, if applied to our position, comes from a lack of understanding of the full significance of phenomenological hermeneutics, for most certainly there is a quest for truth and there is a basis for determining the validity of an interpretation as against others.

First, let us consider the question of truth. Ricoeur offered one of the most cogent arguments on the question of truth in the interpretation of texts as early as the 1972 seminar on literary theory taught at the University of Toronto and later published with the title of 'Appropriation' (*Hemeneutics and the Human Sciences*, 182–93). The question of truth is tangled up in the subject-object dichotomy. Ricoeur suggests that if we give up the concept of subjectivity and consider the reader as a knowing player in the game of redescription of the world, the impasse will dissolve rapidly, for it soon becomes clear that understanding must be self-understanding, that the truth of the text is in fact the truth of ourselves, or to put it in critical terms, the truth of the literary text is the world that it unfolds in the reader's appropriation.

If the truth is tied to the fourth dimension of the text in my self-knowledge, how can one determine between interpretations, we may ask. This, of course, is a loaded question, loaded in the sense that the issue has been shifted from the reading experience to the critical commentary. To put it very strongly, there is no possible distinction or evaluation between one reading experience and another. But it is quite another matter where there is an implicit or explicit claim of authority and knowledge by the writer of a commentary that is based on the reading experience and is disseminated for the sake of other fellow readers. We are therefore involved with the general issue of the validity of critical statements. It is clear that in critical discourse as in any other pursuit of man there will be a wide range of varied talent and ability used in its execution.

The means that Ricoeur suggests as a basis for the evaluation of the writings of psychoanalysis can be transferred to literary criticism. In summary form they are the following: the critical commentary must have a coherency in keeping with its own stated principles; it must also be able to meet its aims; further, criticism must be of consequence to its readers, that is, perform a useful function for them; and finally, criticism must be written as an intelligible narrative. There is no doubt in anyone's mind that we must make value judgments when dealing with literary criticism, and what Ricoeur has proposed is in fact a general guide to judge all interpreters' performances. Consequently, a critic has as much claim as anyone else to the truth he purports to have discovered in reading a literary text, but his performance in sharing this truth is another matter. It can be coherent, accomplished, consequential, and well written, or it can be wanting in one or all of these respects.

The last issue I shall take up is the domain of inquiry of phenomenological hermeneutics. I do not mean to imply in what I have said to this point that there has been anything like unanimity in the tradition of hermeneutics. Quite the contrary. There have been a number of clear-cut mistakes in approach and there will be many more, but through all of this the lines have been drawn between those who accepted a relational view of man's creativity and those who sought to establish absolutes. Our position is clear: the literary text is indeterminate, the work of art is inexhaustible; and the critical activity is always a new putting-into-play of a text in the experience of appropriation. Some of the critical positions that I reject can be summarized in passing for purposes of clarity in establishing my position.

Literary criticism cannot afford the extreme self-indulgence of the pretension of recovering the genius of the author. Equally mistaken is the attempt to reconstruct the original audience of a text as a basis for proposing a definitive interpretation. In this respect it is quite unfortunate that Gadamer's metaphor of a dialogical relationship has been misconstrued. What Gadamer calls the 'fusion of Horizons' is the convergence of the historical horizon of the text and the horizon of the present that is the reader's. Literary criticism is concerned with the relationship between the text and its readers. The text remains the mediator in the process of the fusion of horizons. The concept of the understanding of the text held by the original audience is a pseudo-solution to the problems of interpretation, for it too is a construct of the contemporary critic. What we have in fact under the guise of the original audience's view is a hypothesis that is based on the critic's attempt to identify with specific elements from the past presented under sanction of historical objectivity. Finally, in my review of opposing positions I must also include the extreme relational position of post-structuralism. The text cannot be subsumed by the finite capacities of understanding of the present reader-critic. It is fallacious to propose that the critic can make of the text what he wills. I believe that this popular contemporary position has not been thoroughly examined, and the process of appropriation through which the reader engages the text remains to be considered by Derrida himself. The making-my-own dialectic of appropriation does not mean the incorporation of a mental image into the reader's experience, nor does it mean that one can make the intentions of another subject one's own, nor does appropriation mean that we glean some inner design supposedly hidden in the text, nor does appropriation mean that I can choose to disregard the formal features of the text and unravel its structure as my whim dictates. The dialectical process of appropriation that is at the very core of literary criticism as I understand it is primarily the projection of a world, a proposal of a mode of being in the world, that the text discloses.

I oppose the idea that the critic projects the *a priori* of his own understanding and interpolates this *a priori* into the text. Quite the contrary; appropriation is the process by which the revelation of new modes of being in the experience of reading the text gives the critic a new capacity for knowing himself. If the power of the text is to be found in its capacity to project a configuration of the world, then it is not the critic who projects himself but the text that projects upon the critic. In this way it can be understood that appropriation is not a taking-hold of the text but rather a response to the text that becomes a commentary rooted in self-understanding. It is because absolute knowledge is impossible that the conflict of interpretations, to paraphrase Ricoeur, is insurmountable and inescapable. We, however, do not mourn the finite character of being-in-the-world but celebrate our participation in the community.

5

The Ontological Status of the Critical Text

In this chapter I want to return to the idea expressed earlier that the aesthetic object must have a recipient in order to be actualized, the painting must have a viewer, the literary text must have a reader, and so on. We also return to the idea that the text as an aesthetic object imposes itself on the reader to such an extent that the intentionality of the text is the guiding force in the reader's aesthetic perception and as such becomes a form of alienation in the reader's experience of the text. By the same token let us recall that the will to make the text one's own, which I have described as appropriation, initiates and maintains the reader's refiguration of world. This world-making is the core of the knowing subject's grasp of reality and thus confronts the text's alienation. The dialectic of reader's appropriation and text's intentionality is the play and interplay that characterizes the text-reader relationship. There should be no confusion between the text as potential experience and the text-reader relationship. The former is an ascertainable set of possibilities and probabilities; the latter is reality. After Derrida we cannot but recognize the radical nature of the supplement to the text. We, however, differ with Derrida in his implicit assessment of the supplement as singular realization for each reader. The ontological status of the text is primarily its capacity to redescribe the reader's world in intersubjective terms and not in a private language.

The task at hand, the last in this book, is to describe the ontological status of interpretation: Where does the critic's work stand? What is its relation to the text on which it comments? What is its relation to the readers of both the literary text and the critical commentary? Does it address us individually or as part of a group of intended readers? Does it presuppose awareness of previous commentators? and finally: Does the interpretation address us in a way different from those of other forms of writing, as for example biography or the literary text itself? These are some of the queries we shall discuss here.

The appropriation of the poem by the critic has already taken place when the critical text is composed. The reading experience has become a self-conscious assessment of understanding; the personal and private significance of experience is transcended, and the critical text enters into an intersubjective refiguration of reality whose primary characteristic is that it not only can be shared but it must be shared, for its very purpose of being is its collective design. We must recognize that there must be a voluntary act by the reader to go beyond the phenomenological or experiential level of the text to the critical text. In other words, the reader must will to become a critic and engage in commentary. Only relatively few readers will want to pursue their consideration of the text through the formal, historical, and experiential into the hermeneutic, although most readers will feel motivated to share their views on a text that has been meaningful and rewarding. For those readers who do choose to comment on the text, the dimensions we have outlined are natural ones that do not need theoretical justification or apology. There is, however, no logical imperative that obliges a commentator to give due attention to the expanded context of the poem as I have outlined it; there is only the overwhelming need to establish a common bond between himself as commentator and his intended readers in the present by an appeal to their common precursors. We have now come to the basic concepts of community and tradition that have been central to this study from the outset.

In spite of the practice of calling interpretations 'readings' of poems, the critical commentary is a very different and distinct ontological phenomenon and cannot be treated as if it were a written transcription of reading a poem. The critical commentary has been written by a member of a specific social linguistic group in a tradition that assigns a functional purpose to such writing and for an intended community of readers. Thus, there is from the outset a design and a purpose to the writing that guide the writer. Most writers of critical commentaries will first attempt to establish a commonality of purpose with their intended audience or at the very least appeal to an assumed need on the part of their readers. This common ground can be established through the restatement of a specific norm of interpretation, as in the case of critics who pursue a predetermined issue of interpretation such as the exposition of a feminist viewpoint; it can also be an ideological norm, as in the case of some Marxist critics; it can also be a formalist program for the realization of a controlled, objective description of the poem; and of course the common ground can also be a shared value-concept such as we find in the quest for the truth or the authentic meaning or the author's intended meaning of the poem. In the least distinguished cases the literary critic meets this need by imposing his personal preferences and thus sets out what is a pseudo-common ground. This type of critic simply demands acceptance of the basis for interpretation through the abuse of personal authority. As we have argued before, true authority must be earned and cannot be demanded. Whatever contribution this kind of critic could have made to the consideration of the specified text or texts is largely reduced, because he has succeeded in isolating himself from the very group with whom he should have sought an identification or commonality of purpose.

In phenomenological hermeneutics the starting point is the consideration of the formal dimension of the poetic text, because the initial aim is to establish a common ground with as many persons as possible within the community of readers of the poem. This step is taken because of the recognition that the objectification of meaning is a necessary instrument of mediation between the critic and his readers. As a mediation, formal description and analysis constitute a heuristic design used to establish a common basis for discussion and not to supplant the poem itself. Nor does this starting point deny that behind it stands the critic's initial appropriation as a critical reader. Whereas the reading experience begins with an encounter and the intuition of meaning as the reader strives to make the text serve his configuration of world and overcome its alien origin, the critical commentary begins with a considered strategy, a design to enable the critic to participate in the community. The former is a quest of discovery, the latter an attempt to join in the ongoing tradition of commentary through a rational set of statements about the text.

Richard Rorty's contemporary pragmatist philosophy apparently misses the point when he links up his exhortation 'to keep the conversation going' with the hermeneutic philosophy of Gadamer and Ricoeur, for the whole point of hermeneutics is that what is said in the commentary is a matter of deep concern to the commentator and to the community; if it is not of consequence, it has failed in its primary aim of participation. Rorty suggests that what is said is of secondary concern, for what matters is to say something. The soap-box orator may defend his right to freedom of speech by merely speaking in public, but the hermeneutic commentator is engaged in the collective configuration and refiguration of the world through his commentary.

The intersubjective dimension of the poetic text as expressed through the commentary is of significance to the community that shares the poetic text, to the authors of such writing as well as to the continuing tradition of commentary on such texts. It should be stated again that intersubjectivity is always and at the same time an individual perception and a communal world-view. In so far as it is a personal world-view the commentary bears the signature and critical identity of the critical writer, and his work of composition, analysis, and interpretation quite naturally establishes the commentary as a mode of recognition of a singular view of relative merit and validity, linked as it is to the critic's talent, learning, and skill. Thus we can ask how the same commentary can stand as a communal achievement if it is based on individual merit. The answer has been outlined by Husserl, Heidegger, Ingarden, and of course Gadamer. We can begin to respond by recalling the phenomenological principle of always returning to the insight that the transcendental subjectivity of being-in-the-world brings about the shared reality that is the intersubjectivity of the world. We belong before we know we exist.

There is a structural solidarity between subject and object that is possible because of the priority of being-in-the world. This solidarity is borne out in an analysis of the textual form, the inquiry into the historicity of text and reader, the examination of the reading experience and the final hermeneutic study.

Although we will not pursue the issue in this book, it is important to recognize that the dialectic of the reader-text ontology is but one facet of the dialectic that is human history. Jurij Lotman's concluding chapter in *The Structure of the Artistic Text* suggests his agreement:

When an artistic text simultaneously enters into many intersecting extra-textual structures and each element of the text enters into many segments of the intra-textual structure, the artistic work becomes the carrier of meanings whose correlations are extraordinarily complex ... any description of one structural level inevitably impoverishes the rich semantics of a text. Such descriptions should, therefore, be regarded as a purely heuristic stage in the study of a text, engendered by the wholly legitimate desire first to work out methods for the precise resolution of simple problems, and then to approach more complex structural descriptions; they are not intended to reduce the artistic text to unambiguous systems and then provide the ultimate interpretation of a work of art. (300)

Perhaps the greatest contribution that an examination of the ontology of the critical text can give to humanistic study lies in the realization that there are no absolutes in human inquiry but there is deep in the human spirit a will to the absolute. Unamuno wrote with characteristic insight on this topic more than seventy years ago in *The Tragic Sense of Life*, where he postulated to a bewildered Spanish public that the only God that exists is the human will that there be a God: 'And the fact is that we sense God less as a superhuman consciousness than as the actual consciousness of the human race, past, present and future, as the collective consciousness of the whole human race ... And this God, the living God, your God, our God is in me, is in you, lives in us, and we live and move and have our being in Him ... And He is in us by virtue of the hunger, the longing we have for Him' (193–5). Unamuno is not advocating either religious atheism or philosophical pragmatism; his argument is that the will-to-the-absolute is a part of the dialectic of self and world and the necessary fiction of world-making. In our terms Unamuno's existentialism describes the dialectic of inquiry that we have characterized as the dialectic between appropriation and the alienating intentionality of the text. The objective of hermeneutic inquiry thus looms before us once again: since we are all caught up in the struggle to be the other and yet retain selfhood, it is only through the examination of our configuration of the world and the refiguration through which we constantly enlarge our universe that we attain self-knowledge as we communicate with others.

Let us now turn to the question of the significance of the commentary within the community, setting aside the personal importance it may have for the critic himself and the pragmatist position that only the act itself is what matters. The substance of the commentary is of consequence to the extent that a shared meaning is possible and that there can be a true exchange and enrichment in the ways of world-making. Another way of saying 'the intersubjectivity of world' is: the sense of reality that is common to the community. At the very heart of this concept we have the relation of language to its counterpart, experience. In semantic inquiry we can only assume the relation of language to reality, but we cannot examine this relation as such. To clarify the problem, once again I turn to Paul Ricoeur's *The Rule of Metaphor*:

Perhaps it will venture a philosophical conclusion unawares, by positing language as a whole and in itself as mediation between man and the world, between man and man, within the self itself. Language then appears as that which raises the experience of the world to its articulation in discourse, that which founds communication and brings about the advent of man as speaking subject.

By implicitly assuming these postulates, semantics takes as its own a thesis of 'the philosophy of language' inherited from von Humboldt. But what is this philosophy of language if not philosophy itself, to the extent that it thinks the relation between being and being-said?

It will be objected, before proceeding any farther, that it is not possible to speak of a relation like this because there is no standpoint outside language and because it is and has always been *in* language that men claim to speak *about* language.

This is certainly true. Yet speculative discourse is possible, because language possesses the *reflective* capacity to place itself at a distance and to consider itself, as such and in its entirety, as related to the totality of what is. Language designates itself and its other. This reflective character extends what linguistics calls meta-linguistic functioning, but articulates it in another discourse, speculative discourse. It is then no longer a function that can be opposed to other functions, in particular to the referential function; for it is the knowledge that accompanies the referential function itself, *the knowledge of its being-related to being.* (303–4)

Therefore, we can now ask: is the commentary of a poem a sharing of the poem or is it something else that is shared, that has come about through the critic's response to the poem? My answer, is that it is both. The commentary shares the poem in so far as it makes it the centre against which the discussion takes place, but the commentary also adds to the poem's polysemic context. At any given point in time the text offers a limited field of possible interpretations and it is in this field that the critic works, but we must not lose sight of the fact that the field of possible interpretations is also in time and is itself changing. Given the philosophical argument of phenomenological hermeneutics, the logic of interpretation through the four dimensions of the text allows us to engage in the discussion of meaning within the field of possible interpretations without falling into the two equally reductionist traps of dogmatism (the text has only one meaning) and scepticism (the text remains beyond any shared meaning). The very nature of the commonality of criticism is to argue for or against an interpretation, to confront interpretations, to arbitrate between conflicting interpretations, to seek a meeting of minds, and to propose a new perspective on the poem. Thus it is that when we ask what it is that the critic has contributed through his writing, we are also asking the more basic question of why he has written about the poem. It is all too frequent that the conflict of interpretations fails to lead to the enriching experience of dialogue, but this is because the question of what has been said about the poem is not understood in the light of why it was written. In other words, in the world of human action, intention is an integral part of work itself. We do not have access to the private intentions of the critic any more than we do to those of the poet, but we must allow the critical text or the poem to become a functional instrument of communication. Both are, above all, products of human design and composition, which carry with them the signs of intentional work.

Neither the social scientist nor the legal scholar would dispute the proposition that the meaning of social phenomena, historical events, and human action, in general, may be interpreted in more than one way with equal validity. Yet when we come to the consideration of the poem, which certainly ranks among the most complex and ambivalent of human creations, we are condemned to oscillate between dogmatism and scepticism. The ontological status of the critical commentary, which I have been describing as that of celebration, suggests that there is a specific plurivocity to poetry, a plurivocity that belongs to the very nature of the meaning of human action. And it is because of this premise that I view criticism as a celebration of the creative difference.

I now turn to the consideration of how it is that the critical commentary achieves its ontological status; in other words, how does the commentary celebrate the poem without imposing closure? Earlier I wrote of the text to be studied as a frame of reference for the commentary, as an area of operations wherein lay the potential to transfer any word from the reserve of semantic capacity that we call the dictionary to the particular subset that determines a flexible range of possibilities. The critic enters the textual frame of reference and can bring to it a means of inquiry that applies a heuristic construct we call structure; this is primarily developed on the syntagmatic and paradigmatic axis of linguistics and is clearly an abstract critical construct. The basis for the linguistic axis comes from the observation that when a speaker generates a grammatical phrase in any natural language, he performs two distinct acts: he combines words to make chains that are semantically and grammatically marked as correct idiomatic expressions; and the speaker also selects from among a certain set of terms the ones that are used in any given sentence. The situation becomes more complex in the conjunction of textual segments, the consequent formation of additional meanings in accord with established systems of internal recoding, and the equation of segments coming together in a text, which transform the previously stable elements into a dynamic process of communication in the reader's configuration of meaning. Thus it is that the critic imposes analytical means to postulate the basis for the perceived mechanics of the written text. Two observations are in order here: first, similarity is revealed against the background of diversity and diversity is only visible in the similarity of meaning; and secondly, conjunction and selection as internal systems of recoding vary greatly among different texts, making generalization a most hazardous enterprise. Thus it is that the formal analysis of a text is above all a hypothesis for the examination of composition that postulates that a text is constructed with two types of relations: the contrast and opposition of repeated equivalent elements and the contrast and opposition of adjacent non-equivalent elements.

The text as we have said is taken as a specially organized system that can contain an exceptionally high concentration of contextual information. If we should compare a sentence of ordinary conversation with a poem, we cannot but recognize that the poetic composition can contain and convey a volume of information that is far beyond the capacity of idiomatic speech. The point to be made is that whereas the possibilities of variation in meaning in speech are limited and can soon be exhausted, the range of the poem far exceeds the capacity of the individual speaker. Thus it is that I am basically in agreement with the second generation of Russian Formalists, who hold that the volume of information in a message should be seen as the function of the number of possible alternative messages. The poetic text has, in practical terms, a limitless number of boundaries that break it up into segments that are equivalent in only certain respects and consequently can be regarded as potential alternatives. I have taken up a review of the formal considerations of the poetic text at this point because it is in my view the means of establishing the commonality of criticism, but it is necessary to move beyond analysis into the making of the critical commentary.

It will be recalled that we have emphasized that in passing from the author-text relationship of composition to the reader-text relationship of the configuration of the text, additional alternative possibilities of meaning come into the range of realization. The measure of indeterminacy grows considerably as we enlarge our inquiry from the intentionality of composition to the reading experience, and accordingly the information emanating from the text is much greater. This move from the semiotic and semantic levels of discourse to the experiential is of course basic to our project and is contested by most formalist and historicist critics. The indeterminacy and the amount of possible alternative meaning can be said to grow as interpretative possibilities only if there is a means of accounting for the reader's contribution and of sharing it with others. This is, of course, the function and justification for the critical commentary in phenomenological hermeneutics. It follows logically that if the primary function of criticism is to expand the text and not to limit it, the basic task is to find the means of linking the critical text's contribution to the storehouse of textual commentary that we know as the tradition of criticism.

The ontological status of the commentary as celebration of the text is realized only if the commentary provides the essential energy for the generation of reflective knowledge. Consider an analogy; let us take the tradition of critical commentary as a pre-existing power source much like the electric power system we have today. When a new generating source is being developed, it first takes energy out of the system but ultimately contributes a net gain in energy. Thus the commentator must first plug into the critical tradition and thereby conduct the current through the text, thereby illuminating his own knowledge of the text and in so doing ultimately generating a commentary that adds to the power source of the tradition. We must not, however, confuse the lighting up of the text, the critical study, with the generation of power that is the commentary. The former is a use of the energy source, much like a lamp turning energy into light, and the latter is the production of energy by a new generator. We must also take care not to confuse the light given off by the lamp, which is the reading experience and is the potential for intersubjective participation, with the lamp itself, which is merely the critical means for transforming energy to light. The reader who succeeds in casting light on the text can become the commentator if he writes and thereby contributes a new source of energy to the power source. The written critical commentary has only one major task, and that is to add to the tradition of commentary a shared meaning for other readers present and future.

The process can be misunderstood as when the reading experience is confused with the mere critical vehicle; but of more consequence, the process can be terminated when the critic begins to promote his relatively minor contribution as the only source of energy. This destructive force is of course self-destructive, since the tradition of commentary is a commonality of inquiry. There can be no short-cut; the production of a critic must never be taken as more than a construction whose aim is always to add to the tradition. The contribution of the commentator is not in his device, but only in the shared meaning he generates as a celebration of the poem.

Drawing upon the writings of Unamuno, Gadamer, and Ricoeur as well as Croce and Collingwood, I now turn to the concept of tradition, which heretofore has been implicit in the entire enterprise but has not been addressed directly. In order to establish the concept of tradition as the raison d'être of commentary, I must return to the hermeneutic premise of the dialectical tension between the other and the self. This dialectical concept stands as a rejection of the isolated and alternative opposites of absolute other and absolute self, and in its place proposes an ongoing relationship. The objectification of the other is possible only by the suppression of oneself, and the premise of absolute knowledge purports to stand independently of the knower. However, the absolute self is locked into a closed prison of his consciousness. We exist neither in closed worlds nor within a world that is unique to us. No world is closed, since it is possible to place oneself in another point of view and in another culture. No world is unique, since the continuous tension between the other and oneself is a fundamental[1] feature of the world-making process.

But if this dialectic is a continuous relationship, can it not be said that the idea of a tradition as a huge merger of knowledge is contradictory? This apparent contradiction stems from the assumption that a tradition of inquiry must be taken in a Hegelian sense, wherein individual inquiry is transformed into a cumulative body of knowledge. The fundamental antipathy of contemporary hermeneutics to Hegelian philosophy of history lies in the rejection of absolutes. The individual scholar is never free of his subjectivity. He is always endowed with the full weight of his formation in cultural prejudgment; this fundamental characteristic is his historical present, to which he is unalterably bound. The dialectical relationship that exists between the self and the other is a dynamic movement whereby I am able to place myself in the other's point of view, and furthermore it is only by so doing that I am able to distinguish and recognize the unique nature of my own perspective. To sum up, therefore, it is the struggle (Unamuno) or tension (Ricoeur) between the self and the other that gives us an understanding of the encounter of the text from within my point of view. The encounters of the past serve as a continuing action of inquiry, the debate of shared meanings, which we have called a tradition of commentary. Participation in the tradition is the responsibility of scholarship, which no scholar can dismiss or disregard without making his writing futile.

This common cause of scholarly endeavour cuts across the disciplines we call the humanities, but achieves the unified focus of a tradition when three key factors converge: a common subject matter; accessibility of commentary from the past and from one specialization to another (for example, the history of Spain in the time of Philip II and the philosophy of Spanish Erasmists); and a significant relevance of the work done in the specializations for each other.

There are above all two modes of inquiry that constitute the foundation of a humanistic tradition, and these are history and philosophy. The first is the root discipline of cultural identity; the second provides the spirit of critical inquiry. To paraphrase Croce, each without the other is a lifeless corpse, and every piece of real thinking relates one to the other. The critical examination questions all aspects of the past including society, art, and politics, as evidenced in the present. The interaction between history and philosophy across the last five hundred years has created a vast network of issues and viewpoints. Historical commentary without a sense of critical inquiry can be dismissed as superficial; and similarly, philosophical examination without the awareness of the past significance of human action can be rejected as irrelevant.[2] This is not a new idea, for it has developed continuously from the Renaissance to our day. R.G. Collingwood sums it up aptly: 'The history of thought, and therefore all history, is the re-enactment of past thought in the historian's own mind' (*Idea of History*, 215).

The specific tradition with which I am concerned on these pages – I must select one in order to move the argument to the practical domain of writing commentary – is Hispanic studies, and this tradition of scholarship has been characterized to an extraordinary measure through the union, opposition, and reunion of two very strong intellectual directions: objectification and speculation. At times the systematic collecting of data has been stressed without the scholar's delving into the significance of the data itself; there have also been times when commentary in the Hispanic world was pressed towards speculation about the nature of existing phenomena without the commentator's taking into account the reality of past experience. But the presentation of these extreme positions has primarily served to bring the two extremes closer together with greater vigour than had existed before and to engage the commentator in the debate that characterizes Hispanic studies.

Some of the great Hispanists of the past have made a contribution to the tradition from the one direction looking at the other – Menéndez Pidal and Ortega y Gasset are notable examples – but there has also been another type of Hispanist, scholars who have felt the need of bringing together in their own work the full impact of historical research and critical thought. María Rosa Lida was such a scholar. She was a writer of overwhelming erudition whose work is both history and philosophy as well as literary criticism. From the extensive bibliography of books, monographs, and articles she wrote before her tragic death, it is not easy to discover how she arrived at the integration of historical knowledge and critical thought, but there are a few places where the flawless, seamless garment of her writing does permit us to gain some insight into her method. One of these places is the first paragraph of her book *Two Spanish Masterpieces: The Book of Good Love and The Celestina*:

All students of the *Book of Good Love* and *The Celestina* agree that these are two masterpieces, but they disagree on virtually everything else. For this reason we should keep in mind something so obvious that it is likely to be forgotten: namely, that literary criticism – like all humanistic disciplines – cannot aspire to absolute truth, but rather to a relative and provisional truth within the limitations of the present state of knowledge. What I aspire to expound is not the truth; it is my truth, or, to put it less rhetorically, it is the opinion which I have reached after spending many years carefully considering these two books and examining whatever I have been able to read about them. (1)

This is the language of a pluralist, to whom all claims to knowledge are temporary, to be superseded by others in due course. Nevertheless, there is also the strength of conviction that comes only with the fullest command of the historical data. Her 'relative and provisional truth' is tempered by the, 'many years [spent] carefully considering these two books.' Interpretation is always an individual attempt to understand the whole of the phenomenon under consideration, and in making the attempt the interpreter himself may acquire a better understanding of himself.

There are found in María Rosa Lida's statement clear indications that help us to recover the philosophy of study she practised: 1 / the commentator offers an interpretation of texts that is grounded in his ability, knowledge, and training; 2 / the humanistic disciplines share certain fundamental characteristics: they are interpretative disciplines that examine empirical data from the past; 3 / every commentator works within specific limitations of the present state of knowledge that are beyond the control of the individual; 4 / there is a requirement that one consider all the evidence available before attempting an interpretation. Together these four precepts serve to underscore the interaction between historical scholarship and critical inquiry within a tradition of study marking out a specific area of humanistic achievement, in this case, Hispanic studies.

Philosophy in the Hispanic world has had a long-standing involvement with artistic expression and with the appreciation of the arts. Criticism in Hispanic studies derives from philosophy, but is also linked to history. Criticism is characterized by certain practices that can be described as generally followed throughout contemporary scholarship. There is first the belief in insight as a means of acquiring knowledge. This belief is especially valued by literary critics and less by historians, although it is not altogether absent from their work. The second characteristic is the search for unity or the whole of the phenomenon under consideration. The third characteristic is the elaboration of systems of generalization to respond to historical concepts – for example *Historia como sistema* (Ortega y Gasset), *España como preocupación* (Dolores Franco), *España como problema* (Laín Entralgo). Criticism in Hispanic studies is inextricably entwined with history. In this case a tradition of study emerges through the interaction of the philosophical thrust of inquiry and the historical reconstruction of the past.

The appreciation of insight as a means of acquiring knowledge has had its fullest expression by Benedetto Croce. In the *Aesthetics* Croce distinguishes two forms of knowledge, the intuitive and the logical. The intuitive, he argues, is governed by the imagination in the perception of the individual, in the knowing of individual things. By contrast, logical knowledge is governed by the intellect in its search for universals and the relations among them.

A corollary to intuition as knowledge is that the work of art is a whole. This idea was also given expression by Croce when he held firmly to the concept of the indivisibility of the literary work of art. In Croce's view, if the work of art is perceived, it is perceived because it has unity. In his theory artistic expression is a synthesis of the various and of the multiple in the one. The great value in reading Croce's *Aesthetics* is that in the most extraordinary manner his views are not prescriptive with regard to Hispanic studies, but they most certainly are descriptive of certain basic traits that have been dominant for some three hundred years.

The third generalization we made concerns the Hispanic need to regenerate the past in the present. I know of no other culture that has been so obsessed with its history as a problem. This does not mean that there are unexplored areas in the cultural past but rather that the writers of each generation must find their place within a cultural past that beckons and threatens. Thus the insight of the artistic work of art and the articulation that follows as the unity of achievement is in the process of being explained. It must be finally and ultimately placed into a historical context of a past that will not remain stable because it is constantly under re-elaboration by the literary critic. It is important at this point to emphasize that in these remarks there is no reference to the national origin or place of residence of Hispanists; I am elaborating a general perspective of criticism in Hispanic studies as it is practised on an international basis.

Hispanic culture has its origins in the peninsula, but it has been fused with American, African, and Asiatic strains and is studied everywhwere in the world.

History as a discipline is also in need of some further reflection. The historian must clothe the innate data of the past with as much detail as possible. This act of the educated imagination is done using the experience of the present world as evidence of its own past. Every aspect of the present is grounded in a past of its own, and the very birth of understanding is the imaginative reconstruction of what came before. The historian is fully planted in the present, in which the act of imagination is going on. In this present the impact of the perceived here and now can never be overestimated. The aim of the historical imagination is to utilize the fullest spectrum of perception as the starting point for the building of the past through which it has come to be. It is therefore a return to the headwaters of present experience. As plausible as this all sounds, it can never be fully achieved. The present cannot be grasped in its entirety, and all interpretation is chained to a perspective. The process of development from the present to the past can never be known as a whole, for all our efforts to know are determined by our individual point of view. The fact that objective history is impossible is only to say that it is a human endeavour like art, science, or philosophy.

R.G. Collingwood in his philosophy of history gives us a viewpoint very similar to the statement we cited from María Rosa Lida:

My historical review of the idea of history has resulted in the emergence of an answer to this question: namely, that the historian must re-enact the past in his own mind. What we must now do is to look more closely at this idea, and see what it means in itself and what further consequences it implies.

In a general way, the meaning of the conception is easily understood. When a man thinks historically, he has before him certain documents or relics of the past. His business is to discover what the past was which has left these relics behind it. For example, the relics are certain written words; and in that case he has to discover what the person who wrote those words meant by them. This means discovering the thought ... which he expressed by them. To discover what this thought was, the historian must think it again for himself.

Suppose, for example, he is reading the Theodosian Code, and has before him a certain edict of an emperor. Merely reading the words and being able to translate them does not amount to knowing their historical significance. In order to do that he must envisage the situation with which the emperor was trying to deal, and he must envisage it as the emperor envisaged it. Then he must see for himself, just as if the emperor's situation were his own, how such a situation might be dealt with; he must see the possible alternatives, and the reasons for choosing one rather than another; and thus he must go through the process which the emperor went through in deciding on this particular course. Thus he is re-enacting in his own mind the experience of the emperor; and only in so far as he does this has he any historical knowledge, as distinct from a merely philological knowledge, of the meaning of the edict. (*Idea of History* 282–3)

Unlike technology, which is strictly progressive, with each new development making its precursor obsolete, a cultural tradition stays alive only if it constantly renews itself. Hispanic studies, like all great traditions of mankind, fosters a certain sense of history that is both cumulative and innovative. Whereas nations develop their culture by establishing modes that are observed and that are recognized as belonging together, the observance of the past cannot choke off renewal and recreation or the culture will die. Every generation needs writers, thinkers, and artists to challenge the old in order to save it from becoming empty ritual. Hispanic civilization demonstrates above all how there can be a tradition of rebels who have been willing to risk all again and again with inventiveness and a sense of adventure. The literary artist, like all artists, gives an expression of his civilization only if he does not intend to be a national voice and if no one authorizes him as spokesman. What I am writing about Hispanic studies is not unique to it, but it is dramatically evident in all periods of Hispanic writing on both continents and in four languages. If political authority could direct the poet to 'create culture,' this order would have to be put in the language of technology, and it could only be understood and followed in the same mode. Much verbal technology abounds which as creation is false. We who study the Hispanic tradition can only know after the fact if the artist has been successful in taking the fundamental, familiar images that have made Hispanic civilization and giving them a new guise. Each time a new creation is born and we are able to recognize both its roots and its thrust, we will also be able to project and anticipate the direction in which the tradition is going. Hispanic artistic creations abound in a sense of the outrageous. Many of the contemporaries of Cervantes, Góngora, Quevedo, El Greco, Feijoó, Larra, Goya, Bécquer, Unamuno, Picasso, Valle-Inclán, García Lorca, Cela, and Goytisolo were shocked by the scandal of their daring. The false, self-complacent images a people likes to indulge in need to be shattered. It is necessary to have an artistic shock to our sensibilities. Any group that dominates the political and economic power of the state will want to be given a favourable image. The artist, being a non-conformist in his own milieu, will aim at the destruction of this rose-coloured mirror. The Hispanic artist often stands in solitude, in contention, and feeling himself misunderstood and always misused by society; he creates works of art that are both bewildering and shocking to their first recipients, but these are works that form part of that most unique of civilization, in which each generation feels compelled to devour its past in order to create its present, which will in turn be the repast of a future generation.

Hispanic studies has its pragmatic focus on the study of literary documents as works of art. When Menéndez Pelayo (1856–1912) set about to co-ordinate a general history of Spanish literature, there was never any doubt that the starting point was the analysis of the texts themselves. In spite of eclectic methodology or lapses in research, the program itself has not been in doubt. For it is clear to anyone who knows the Hispanic world that before we can write a literary and artistic history of this tradition and before we can interpret the reasons for and the why of cultural works, we must have an overview of the specific texts that embody the tradition. It is clearly insufficient to have an inventory of authors, titles, and period characteristics as so much raw material. The contradictory nature of the Hispanic tradition obliges us to penetrate into the significance of each text. In brief, we must understand what it has to say to us about itself, about the past, and about us. The process of gaining an understanding is a demanding one that has varied over the years as critics have placed more relative emphasis on one of three related aspects of the tradition: the text itself, the past, or we the interpreters. But whether philological, historical, or hermeneutic, the imperative is the same: the texts are the foundation of all further commentary on history and form. When as a result of commentary the discussion begins to give way to clearer, more specific understanding, both historical relations and basic forms begin gradually to emerge as distinguishable units. As work progresses, certain classes of texts group themselves together, and we begin to discover orderings and relationships within these classes. At this point we are at the threshold of literary history; this task, one of the dominant concerns of Hispanic studies, is in fact causal knowledge. What literary history affirms is not that we have recovered the whole of the tradition but rather that knowledge of causal relationships does not exhaust the reality of Hispanic civilization, for the texts themselves are inexhaustible. A kind of dead-end looms before us only if we have been under the impression that the concepts of cause and effect are the only guides to knowledge and that if they should fail to exhaust the subject matter, only obscurity will remain. This epistemological trap has led contemporary critics into extreme scepticism. The either-or dilemma they have been victims to has come about because they have not been able to respond to the challenge of literary history. What has continually impeded and held up acceptance of the multiple dimensions of knowledge has been the idea of progress, which has only been with us for some two hundred years. The causal knowledge of literary history does not deal with fixed or permanent truth; it is the essential cultural interpretation of the past that must be redone by each new generation, who will find new aspects of the great works of the past.

The study of texts and the writing of history are fruitful and necessary enterprises, but they do not cover the full scope of Hispanic studies as a tradition. If we recognize that the monuments of the tradition like the *Libro de buen amor*, the *Celestina, Don Quixote*, and the *Buscón* are inexhaustible sources that are renewed by each generation of readers and scholars, there remains the fundamental question of accounting for what is permanent amidst the change in readers' perspectives. To use a metaphor that has been with us from Garcilaso to Borges, we attain knowledge of man by viewing man in the mirror of his civilization. We read, study, and comment on the work of art; we pursue these readings in a causal quest as we seek to enlarge our view of man by placing him in history, and finally we recognize that history is but a recognition of the mirror and its frame. The reflected images change with the perceiver and the mirror itself has a tendency to fluctuate markedly, but through the flux we also recognize some characteristics and traits that are repeated with variations again and again. The repetitions are the symbolic forms that Hispanic civilization has evolved, and these must also be examined as the culmination of the scholarly process.

Hispanic studies is today one of many communities of participants in a common intellectual and scholarly endeavour – in this case, the study of Hispanic culture. Unlike Borges's sect of the phoenix there is no ritual, but neither is there a common book of scripture. What sustains the community is a tradition of commentary. In the preceding pages I have attempted to sketch the specific mode of inquiry that characterizes this community. I have also sought to emphasize that every critical text written for this community draws from the tradition that has formed and maintains the commonality of the community. My entry into the details of a specific example has been made necessary, in my view, because of the general nature of my earlier remarks on community and tradition.

In conclusion, therefore, the two pre-conditions for the critical text are that it be addressed to a specific community and that it participate in a tradition of inquiry. The ontological status of the critical text is that of being the well-spring of the dialectic of belonging to the world that embodies the tension between the critic's appropriation of the poem and the alienating distanciation of the poetic text. The critical text as well-spring is a celebration of the life of the mind.

PART III

Celebrations

There are two related questions that are sometimes confused: what is literature, and what is a literary text? The first question is a historical one with a body of historical documentation that enables us to determine what the concept of literature meant at a specific time and in a particular culture and language. The other question is philosophical, and it goes to the very heart of the reader-text relationship. I am here concerned with the latter. In my theory a literary text is any written work that has the capacity to provoke the redescription of the world by its reader.

This concept of the literary text gives a new sense of purpose and of responsibility to literary criticism. The route to revision and expansion of a reader's life-world is made possible primarily by the written text. Therefore the redescription of the world through literature represents man's liberation from the circumstances of time and space. The commentary on this power of language to transcend the immediate circumstances of both wtiter and reader is a celebration of the life of the mind, to borrow Hannah Arendt's apt phrase. And far from being a licence for the critic to indulge himself or herself in self-gratification and empty self-congratulation, it renders the literary critic's task both heavier and more deeply meaningful. Writers in Africa, Asia, Europe, and Latin America know full well of what I call the burden of self-truth. It is only in some corners of academic North America that trivialization has taken over critic's minds.

In this third part I propose to demonstrate what heretofore has been a sustained theoretical discussion. What does it mean in terms of what we do as critics when I repeatedly stress that the basic aim of criticism, whatever other claims the critic may choose to make notwithstanding, must be the edification of the critic himself and of his readers through participation in the community of commentary that can be traced back to the *studia humanitatis* of the Renaissance. I have selected two texts for commentary, the first a fragment of a very long poem, the coda or first and last six verses of *Piedra de sol* by Octavio Paz. This 584-verse poem was first published in Mexico by Tezontle in 1957, and the following year it was included in *La estación violenta*. The translation is my own. My second text is 'La secta del Fénix' by Jorge Luis Borges. It was published in 1956 as part of the expanded republication of *Ficciones*. The English translation I am using is by James E. Irby and was first published in *Labyrinths*.

6

Critical Commentary on the Coda of
Piedra de sol by Octavio Paz

Our first commentary is on the configuration of poetic meaning in the coda of *Piedra de sol* / *Sun Stone* by Octavio Paz.[1] Consider the word *sauce* (willow); in ordinary usage it refers to a certain class of trees. If we agree on this much, we assert that there is a relation between the word *sauce* (willow) and an identifiable part of the flora of North America. But when we read *sauce* (willow) in a poem, does the original relation still obtain? Consider the following line: 'un sauce de cristal' (a crystal willow). It is this relation that is the object of this inquiry.

Let us first turn to the dictionary and establish what sort of thing a word is and for the moment leave aside the issue of its status in a poem. To begin with there are a number of projected usages with precedents recorded in the lexicon, and secondly there are an undetermined number of usages that cannot be projected but that are part of the theoretical potential of the development of language. At any given point in actual usage a word has a range of expression of all the different occasions when it can be employed in meaningful communication. A word in the dictionary is not the name of an object; it is a lexical subsystem of communication.

If I say the word *sauce* (willow) to someone, it has an intentional function to perform in conveying meaningful communication to my listener; it is an utterance with implicit meaning that the listener must grasp if he is to understand the message. But the possibility of uttering a single word without an implicit context is not only remote; it is contrary to the basic functional needs of speech, for the intentional function only exists within a context of communication, and similarly the decoding function only exists in the implicit situation of a communicative context.

A single word therefore is a lexical subsystem for communication. The utterance of a word is the activation of the subsystem within a specific context that controls and directs the possibilities of communication, reducing a potential myriad to a relatively small number of variations that perform under the specific constraints of the context. In our example we have very clear contrasts in usage, dictated by context. Thus if the context is botanical, the word *sauce* will refer to a member of the genus *Salix*; if the context is botanical but with usage less rigorous than accurate description, the word can be the name of willow-like plants; in a specific context of human relations the word can symbolize lost love; in a context of playing cricket *willow* will be used as a synecdoche for the cricket bat; and even more remote from the above is the context of cotton-processing, where the word refers to a machine used for cleaning the fibre of the cotton plant.

The following points have been made: first a word entry in a dictionary serves to establish the principal aspects of usage from the lexical subsystem, which is itself a record of previous usage; and second, a word in an utterance has a specific context that establishes a designated area of usage and thus excludes all others.

Let us now consider the problematic issue of meaning for the written word. When I write the word *sauce* in a sentence, I have placed it in a context, an activity similar to what I do with words in speaking but with the essential difference that the assumed common situation between speakers is absent in writing. I must substitute for voice, gesture, and appearance through a symbolically created situation that cannot be assumed. I can choose to elaborate the context or to keep it open and indeterminate, but whatever I choose, I have a degree of control in the creation of the context. What I do when I write is to elaborate a system that will control and direct the use of words that most closely transmits my intentions, but I am always stopped short of complete control because I have no way of ensuring that my written system will be grasped fully by the reader. The issue here is not one of isomorphic transference, since it could very well be the writer's intention to transmit an ambiguous statement that is not recognized as such by the reader. Writing reaches the reader as intentionality contained within a system. The reader must appropriate the signs and create a context. The point here is that the reader's created context is not the same as the writer's. The signs are the same, but the activating of the signs depends on the reader's own systems and his capacity to respond to other systems. Thus there are two different contexts for the same word: the writer's and the reader's.

In considering what writing means, it is therefore necessary to start with the premise of two contexts, only one of which is available to any person, be he writer or reader. In the case of a written commentary on someone else's writing the commentator must begin with the context he created as a reader and can if he is so inclined speculate about the context of the writer he is examining. Nevertheless, the commentator should be aware that the entire process is duplicating itself, as he is now a writer who will presumably have a reader.

Passing on to poetry, we enter into a conventional system of signs that is bound up with a tradition of texts. This observation does not supersede our earlier comments, for the intertextuality of a poetic text does not reveal the writer's context; intertextual relations do not function as a set of signs for the reader to create into a context. The tradition serves as a common background to both writer and reader as well as to commentator and the commentator's reader, but it does not supplant the creation of context. Poetic configuration is a continuing affirmation born out of a continuing negation. The textual signs affirm images because they deny literal associations. The reader's context is created within the force-field of this affirmation and negation.

The hypothesis for the phenomenological study of literature is that the configuration of poetic meaning is deeply rooted in our experience and understanding of the world of action. By the world of action let us understand the distinctive structure of the world's temporal features. In terms of literary criticism this hypothesis, if valid, would mean that no interpretation is possible without grounding in a theory of action, or, in other words, that all referential poetic activity is based on whatever it is we understand as constituting human action. The specific intelligibility generated by a poetic text grows out of the reader's experience of human action.

I recognize that my argument is now dangerously close to falling into a circular trap. Could it not be argued that the experiential ground that I claim for poetic configuration was planted in my experience of the world, for the world as we know it is already mediated by the cultural structures of language, social institutions, and conventions? In other words, I know what I know about the world through a continuous stream of linguistic intermediaries. Therefore, if having experience is, in at least some rudimentary sense, a linguistic formulation of images, figures of speech, metaphors, and, of course, narrative, is not memory itself organized through a kind of text? The implications are varied and significant. Are we to understand that the world, as we know it, is so because of forms of discourse? A formless recollection would be unintelligible. In answer to this argument we can say that human action may be organized by the form of discourse to the extent that the action in question is *rule-governed* activity. There is, however, a wide range of activity that is not rule-governed. Consequently, it is clear that we are not following a circular argument, for what I have been proposing is that the written text is knowable because it draws from the world-view we have received through the organizational means of cultural language-forms. This does not preclude the generation of an incessant flow of mutations by the rich diversity of individual experience. To this point Paul Ricoeur writes: 'To understand a rite is to situate it first within a ritual; to situate the ritual within a particular cult, and then step by step within the whole of conventions, beliefs, and institutions which form the network or the fabric of culture.'[2]

The insight gained for our argument is that poetic texts are complex systems of referentiality that I can best describe in terms of three levels of activity. The first is the reflective capacity of the text to echo the informal logic of real life: trees have roots, branches and leaves; rivers have running water and their course in time meanders over the land. The first level thus holds that the text is always produced against the background of the experiential essence of cultural identity. The second level of the text is the formal means used to organize the configuration. The third level is the capacity of the text to redescribe life for the reader. If the ultimate function of a text is to redescribe life, that function makes sense to me only to the extent that there is a symbolic system that provides a context of description for individual actions. Therefore, we take a given behaviour as having a specific meaning only in terms of symbolic law. The gesture of clasping another's hand and shaking it vigorously functions as a symbol of greeting only because of a controlled code of usage that includes position, environment, circumstances, and so on. In this sense the greeting symbol is a rule for interpreting certain empirical actions. Action is meaningful only because of the symbolism that allows its interpretation. The poetic text is human action symbolically mediated; it is readable because it draws on the experience of real life, whether to enhance, negate, or violate, but it is always a return to the human act.

The poet's writing is transformed into the reader's created context through a dialectical relationship that ultimately is the subject of study for us. The text stands with a history and a tradition, but independent of its writer. The reader engages the text, which is distant and alien to his experience, and then proceeds to appropriate it. The initial distance between the text and the reader is never overcome; the activity of 'making mine' is the struggle to overcome this distance. Within this dynamic relation a context emerges, and it is the making of the context that we seek to describe. The only access I have to the created context is an examination of the one I have created as a reader, but it is my aim to describe more than the specific characteristics of my created context: my aim is to outline the basic traits of the reader's context of a poetic text. I have alluded to the traits of context in the preceding commentary; these are: the formal structures of the text, which serve as the perimeters of action (appropriation); the repertoire of iconicity and poetic language, which exists as part of the tradition of poetic writing and of culture itself; the appropriation of symbol and metaphor as the means of aesthetic augmentation of reality, which is the essence of poetic meaning; and the critical self-assessment.

Coda

Un sauce de cristal, un chopo de agua,
Un alto surtidor que el viento arquea
Un árbol bien plantado mas danzante,
Un caminar de río que se curva,
avanza, retrocede, da un rodeo
y llega siempre

A willow of crystal, a poplar of water
A high spouting jet arched by the wind
A well-rooted yet dancing tree
A movement of river which curves
advances, moves backward, goes
round and always arrives

These lines constitute the coda or formal close of Paz's poem. They return full circle to the opening and reiterate the metaphor that controls the vast network of signs and symbols throughout the 584 lines of the poem. The coda serves first as the threshold into the cycle of self-discovery, but it must also replace an ending 573 verses later and give the poem the impetus for the renewal of the cycle, which is continuous. The coda is therefore a powerful means of entry and re-entry into the cyclical world of metaphors, which transcends the 'I-you' encounter of the lyric voice and attains an 'I am you' and 'You are I' within the discovery of 'we are.'

FORMAL STRUCTURES OF THE TEXT

The verse form of perfect eleven- and five- syllable lines establishes a remarkable sound pattern that reinforces a syntactical rhythm through the subtle regularity of the stress pattern. The smooth flow of sounds, with its even-numbered cadence of stresses, gives the coda movement in two tempos. The first three verses are marked with perfect eleven-syllable regularity, with the stress on the even-numbered syllables. The fourth to the sixth verses, by contrast, render a syncopated variation by omitting some of the accents, thus producing a continuous flow through the twenty-seven syllables.

The first verse presents a specific structural relation of contrasting parallels: 'un sauce de cristal' is set in a parallel relation to 'un chopo de agua.' The words 'sauce' (willow) and 'chopo' (poplar) belong to the same set of *tree*, thus reinforcing the syntactical parallelism. Two trees and their attributes are named in strict sequence in the same line. The contrast emerges with the attributes of the trees. Both 'cristal' and 'agua' defy the literal attributes of the class *tree*; thus there is an immediate contrast between the class attributes that are absent and the new attributes that appear in negation of the absent but implicit attributes. What emerges is a special relationship of the words 'cristal' and 'agua' since they share the formal position of attributes of the class *tree* and the negation of the botanical attributes. This special relationship thus gives a distinct focus to the two words that enhances their syntagmatic place. When they are cast as a pair of poetic terms, implicit shared features of each are put into play, features such as transparency and coolness and dissimilar features such as solid and liquid are submerged into the basic contrastive aspect of the poetic trees and botanical trees.

The stanza offers us another formal relationship of terms, which is seriation. Five terms – 'sauce,' 'chopo,' 'surtidor,' 'árbol,' and 'caminar' – are presented in a serial structure preceded by the article 'un,' all within the space of four lines. On closer examination we find that the series of terms preceded by the article (distinctive mark of seriation) progresses in an intricate pattern of intensifying abstraction. The first two terms are botanical terms that have been jolted from their established lexical place in the system because of the attributes 'cristal' and 'agua.' The third term is the metaphorical embodiment of the first two terms as tree and fountain are merged in creative tension. The fourth term restates the metaphor as the well-rooted yet dancing tree. The metaphorical intensification of the series from willow and poplar to tree and fountain is not only a movement from individual to genus but also from conflict to metaphor. Finally, with the culmination of the series in the fifth term, we encounter the verbal noun 'un caminar,' and we not only focus on motion but also engage in the metonymic substitution of an attribute (motion) for the image (dancing tree) and then conclude the series by an unexpected analogy to another water image, the aerial view of a river: 'Un caminar de río que se curva, avanza, retrocede, da un rodeo y llega siempre' The series itself culminates like a river in the breakthrough of the river analogy. We shall return to the structure of analogy.

There is another formal structure evident in these lines besides parallel contrasts and seriation, and this is the simple device of syntactical contradiction, which in this case is an essential part of metaphor. The third line states in the form of a contradiction what has been implicit from the first line – that is, that botanical terms such as *willow* and *poplar* cannot have attributes such as *crystal* and *water*. But it is in the third line that there is the development of the syntactical device of two opposite attributes assigned to the same term with only the negative conjunction 'mas' separating them; 'a tree [that is] well rooted but [nevertheless] dancing' is an acceptable paraphrase of the line 'un árbol bien plantado mas danzante.' The syntactical structure of contradiction serves to make the implicit come to the surface. The preceding image of the water stream arched by the wind has been superimposed on the tree (species and genre) and culminates in the metaphor of water and temporality through the addition of the syntactical contradiction that links the water jet with the dancing tree.

The last formal structure is the analogy created between water jet and river, both in a perceptive field with implicit distanciation. The structure of analogy operates on the basis of position in the text of similar elements that can serve to make the radical leap from one set of terms to another. In this case the linkage is provided by water implicit in 'surtidor' and 'río.' Although we leap from the metaphor of tree-fountain to the set of descriptive terms of the river, this is not a mere passing from one metaphorical image to another, for the focus is not on the river and its properties but rather on motion, time, and perception, just as it has been in the first metaphor. Analogy has structured *river* into the text as another example rather than as a change of direction. The analogy is constructed in this text by the simple device of subordinating the term *river*, so that it cannot rival *tree*. The last two lines of the passage under consideration begin with the completion of the seriation we have discussed and then the attributes of the term *motion*, which now happens to be that of a river instead of the water jet. The power of the analogy fixes the emphasis not on the examples but on the central ideas of motion, time, and perception.

HISTORICITY REPERTOIRE OF PICTORIAL ICONICITY, AND POETIC LANGUAGE

There are two determining pictorial motifs in our text: the Mexican pre-Hispanic tree of life and the aerial view of a river. The tree of life in pre-Hispanic Mexico is depicted as a tree-fountain. At its base the tree is rooted, but the trunk itself is represented as moving water, rushing to the apex where it spreads out to the right and the left as in the outspread branches of the weeping willow. The pictorial symbols are those of opposition overcome through the unification of the stream of water – tree trunk. The intricate symbolism of the tree of life goes back to Teotihuacan civilization (circa 400 AD) and is best depicted in the Borgia codex; the full dimensions of the Nahuatl symbolic language is not the issue here. The pictorial representation of the tree-fountain is that of movement.

The second pictorial motif suggested by the text is a visual representation of relativity gained by distance and the overall perspective. The 'always' of 'siempre llega' – can be conceptualized as the aerial view of the river which is always in motion yet can be seen to curve, advance, return, and curve. The motif is a record of movement. The implicit reference to the two motifs is but part of the general program of pictorial iconicity possible in poetic language. In this case the motifs serve to reinforce the dominant theme of movement in the text. Poetic reference is not fundamentally different from reference in ordinary language. When we read a text the writing has two ways of referring: through description of aspects of the reader's experience and through a formulation or configuration that is new and therefore must be appropriated. In poetic texts the same two modes of reference obtain, but with the notable difference that the two are simultaneous and dialectically related.

When we read: 'sauce de cristal, chopo de agua,' we recognize a reference to classes of trees; without this recognition the line would be meaningless, for it is the position and the relation of the botanical terms within the parallel structure that establishes the opposition for 'cristal' and 'agua.' The referentiality of the contradictory terms is metaphorical and thus adds a new dimension – the idea of the water-tree and the ensuing icon – but the metaphorical relation also refers us back to the text and to textuality and thereby posits its literary dimension. Consequently the metaphorical reference is creative and self-referential at once. The self-referentiality releases the intertextual systems of meaning. Let us consider some of these. The privileged position of 'cristal' and 'agua' evokes Garcilaso de la Vega's

Corrientes aguas, puras, cristalinas
Árboles que os estays mirando en ellas.
(*Égloga primera*, 238–40)

In Garcilaso's lines the running water, pure and crystalline, reflects the trees. Thus the contrast of motion and material appearance of continuity and stability in our text has a significant reinforcement from the text alluded to. Of course the motif of the willow tree by the side of the river is an ancient one, as we can readily recall from Ovid:

I found a stream that smooth and silent ran
Clear to the bottom, so that you could scan
Each pebble there; it hardly seemed to move.
Wild silvery willows shaded it above,
And poplars that by rivers nurtured grow.
(*Metamorphoses* v, 587–91)

Although it is the motif of willow and poplar reflected in the moving water that leads us back to Ovid, there is a more significant connection in the poetic opposition of *transformatio* to *imitatio*. The theme of metamorphosis connects the mythological tales in Ovid's work. The Latin word that corresponds to the Greek word *metamorphosis* is *transformatio*, and transformation is what Ovid's poem is about; a change in shape, usually quite sudden, from human to animal or mineral or divine. In the passage I have cited the water nymph Arethusa has been transformed from human shape into a stream in order to escape her seducer Alpheus, who promptly changes from his male shape back to water in order to mingle with the nymph. The frenzied lover is thwarted only because the goddess can also part the earth and thus transport the nymph's stream. In Octavio Paz's poem the shape of trees is retained, but the attributes of botanical trees are transformed; the image remains while the anticipated attributes of tree are replaced by crystal and water. This is an inversion of Ovid's metamorphosis, where shapes change while attributes such as frenzied love persist. The inverted *transformatio* in Paz rejects *imitatio* as in Ovid and discloses a presence of self rather than of human passions.

But the significant lyrical alchemy of our text is to take the classical motif with its Spanish echoes and to tie it to a Bergsonian metaphor rather than nurture the direction of life and death as Rilke did in his 'Fourth Elegy' of the *Duino Elegies*. The Bergsonian idea of *durée* and his metaphor of the fountain adds another facet to our text. It will be recalled that according to

Henri Bergson we discover the flowing of our personality through time. What this means is not that there is an absolute self but that we discover reality to be a ceaselessly changing process. *Durée* is a heterogeneous flux that is irreversible, jetting always towards becoming; it is continually creating itself, like the head of the fountain always renewed yet apprehensible.

Another poet's lines are suggested in our text. This echo is not through the motif of the trees and the river but through the meditation on time as evoked by the river in Herakleitos and the modern poet of time, T.S. Eliot. Consider these lines from 'Burnt Norton':

Neither from nor towards; at the still point, there the dance is,
But neither arrest nor movement. And do not call it fixity.
Where past and future are gathered. Neither movement from nor towards (I, 18–22)

The pictorial iconic reflection on the river has joined the lyrical tradition of permanence in change, and the lines we read in our text are taken from the repertoire, belong to the repertoire, and add to it. I am not concerned with questions of author's intentions or influences, nor am I interested in making an exhaustive inventory of lyrical relations of reference. My only objective is to underscore that the self-referential aspect of the text is not to an isolated configuration of words and images. The self-referential direction of the poetic language is to the poetic repertoire, without which we would not understand reality. For it is my contention that just as our bodies are the product of the nutrition we have been provided, so is our understanding of reality the product of our repertoire of motifs, images, metaphors, and, of course, narratives.

APPROPRIATION, EXPLANATION, AND UNDERSTANDING

There are several points to be made at this juncture:

1 There is a marked tension between the two forms of reference I have described. This conflict does not diminish, for it is the force behind the metaphorical gain in meaning. The referential direction that leads us to think of botanical properties with the words *poplar*, *willow*, and *tree* is an essential factor in the eventual creation of the metaphor. The denial of botanical properties to these terms and the attribution of alien properties such as crystal and water is also essential. It is the immediate clash and the ensuing tension that produce the creative process of the living metaphor.

2 Tension is the creative power of the metaphor and does not diminish with understanding. We do not move from willow trees to poplar trees to another kind of tree. The poetic referentiality is a split reference that maintains both the trace of the literal reference, which has been discarded, and the metaphorical reference, which is the tree-fountain, and in so doing creates a dialectical tension. The poetic meaning is a net gain, and this is maintained through the continued dialectic between the trees we know and the attributes named in the text, which are unacceptable to trees as we know them.

3 Poetic configuration can thus be characterized as a split form of referentiality in so far as it is continuously referring to experience beyond the text and back to the text as a unique experience.

4 The self-referentiality of poetic language is a complex phenomenon that can be observed as three separate levels of interaction:

- The metaphorical idea is expressed within formal structures whose potential can be examined as a functional capacity.
- The metaphorical idea has iconic implications as well as overt and covert relations to other texts, because it is a cultural product.
- The metaphorical idea can only be realized and actualized by a reader. As form it is potential expression; it is only as a reader's text – that is, as reading experience – that it grasps its reality as expression.

We have discussed formal structures as well as the relations of the text to our cultural pre-understanding, but we have yet to elaborate the process of the appropriation of the text by the reader. The fundamental observation that must be made regarding the reading experience is that the process of appropriation by the reader presupposes a contrary force of separation brought about by the symbolic character of a written text as distinct from a speaker engaged in conversation with another. Thus there is a dialectical relationship in the process of reading as the reader seeks to make the otherness of the text into his own experience. I do not propose that there be a Hegelian synthesis that makes progress a step on the way to absolute knowledge, but I do want to insist on two points: first, the necessity of considering the reading experience as a process, as a dynamic encounter, and second, the resilience of both poles, text and reader, because the process is to be repeated with every reading.

CRITICAL INTERPRETATION

The six lines we have taken as our text in this commentary have been discussed as a formal strategy, as a link to our cultural pre-understanding, and now, if we are to comment on the text's meaning, that is, explain it, we must implicitly claim some understanding of it. But what kind of claim will this be? Let us be clear on the issue. I do not claim that my interpretation has or will have an absolute validity for the text, but neither do I accept that it is or will be a mere subjective rendering of the text based on my personal affinities. My claim is that my interpretation is part of a tradition of commentary dealing with essentially inexhaustible texts. The validity of my interpretation is to be measured within the tradition of commentary (literary criticism) on the basis of its effectiveness, its comprehensiveness, and its lucidity. Before engaging the text in interpretation, I want to recall that we have described the reading experience as a dialectic between the otherness of the text and the need to appropriate it by the reader. In parallel argument the critical act of interpretation is also a dialectic (which comes after the reading experience) whereby we re-establish the otherness of the text by our methodological insistence on form and formal structures as distinct from the memory of my reading experience. As I engage in writing my interpretation I am forced to explain what it is I understand. The critical act or interpretation thus is the last dialectical relationship in a series of such dynamic relationships. I must somehow find the words that explain what I understand the poem to say, presupposing that we (my reader and I) share a number of common factors such as language, culture, critical apparatus, and so on.

Un sauce de cristal, un chopo de agua

The text opens with an image of the water-tree, evoking both the classical motif of the weeping willow by the side of water as well as the pre-Hispanic icon of the tree of life. The basic conflict of the metaphorical statement is already in place – the opposition of change and permanence.

Un alto surtidor que el viento arquea

The metaphor takes a leap forward with the second line as the idea of Bergsonian time is suggested and the opposition of change and permanence becomes involved with the opposition of illusion and reality.

Un árbol bien plantado mas danzante

The hint of the trace of Mexican culture now becomes explicit as the icon of the tree of life of the pre-Hispanic codex comes to the fore. The necessity of the two sides of the contradiction seems to be overwhelming, 'deep-rooted tree' versus 'dancing tree.' The Mexican pre-Hispanic imagination thrives on this type of metaphorical contradiction; we are reminded of a heritage that contains 'burning water' and 'plumed serpent.'

Un caminar de río que se curva,
avanza, retrocede, da un rodeo
y llega siempre

For the second time during the brief span of this text we take a leap, as the specificity of the water-tree and the tree of life are boldly superimposed on the river, which has been marginal, present only by distant implication of the motif of the weeping willow by the side of the river. Not only is the river brought forward as an analogy to other forms of running water, but also to evoke the richness of the river of Herakleitos. Time perception and reality now merge into a metaphor of some consequence. The water fountain appears to have permanence in spite of the fact it is always changing. The river is flux itself when we stand beside it, but when we view it from above, the relativity of time becomes apparent, for its forward motion is in a causeway that is not straight but goes forward, backward, and curves round. Yet on our return to its waters the time is always now, always the present of coming into being, of arriving. The metaphor of time as flux, of reality as flux, and of event as a necessary illusion of human perspective is now complete. This reader has made the full circle from text to experience to formal re-establishment of text to explanation of understanding and finally to the reception of enrichment.

7

Critical Commentary on 'La secta del Fénix' by Jorge Luis Borges

This short text by Jorge Luis Borges (see Appendix) consists of five paragraphs. The first paragraph opens with what appears to be a traditional philological argument challenging the validity of 'those' who write that the sect of the Phoenix had its origin in Heliopolis and who derive this claim from a historical hypothesis based on ancient texts and archaeological conjecture. The philological argument, however, gives way to self-parody, for the counter-argument turns in on itself and destroys its own ground. The main point of philological dissension was the claim that the name 'sect of the Phoenix' could not be traced back to the ancient Egyptian city of Heliopolis because the name is of much later origin (philological evidence); all earlier texts refer only to the 'people of the custom' or the 'people of the secret.' The basis of the philological argument is the implicit connection between the name and the referential entity: sect or people. This assumption, however, is disputed with the proposition that the public name of a group can be different from the name used by the members themselves. Religious groups abound with such nominal discrepancies, which the narrator reminds us is also part of the historical record. Thus it is that the first paragraph cancels itself out; we emerge only with names and with no basis whatsoever for accepting or rejecting the unsupported claims about the origin of the title.

Three names emerge in a synonymic relationship: sect of the Phoenix, People of the Custom, and People of the Secret, but the apparent synonymity turns out to be a frame for a double contradiction. The first term is opposed to the second and third in so far as 'sect' specifies a religious group and 'of the Phoenix' identifies the religious group with a symbolic proper name that is indeterminate. By contrast, both of the other terms designate only a plurality of persons without adding even the minimal identity of class; further, both are non-symbolic and clearly determinate. The synonymic relationship is thus only apparent and comes to nothing more than an arbitrary listing; it does not indicate a logical relationship among the three terms. The second contradiction is more destructive than the first; 'People of the Custom' and 'People of the Secret' cancel each other out. If an act is a custom rather than a ritual, it can only be a secret in a purely nominal manner; that is, some people can choose to consider a custom their secret, but the terms *custom* and *secret* tend to cancel each other out, for customs are transmitted through cultural communities and secrets are held singularly or collectively by particular individuals such as priests.

Midway through the first paragraph the narrator shifts from the third- to a first-person narrative voice. The objections to the philological evidence have rested on the date attributed to 'Phoenix'; as we have seen, this objection is obviated by the dismissal of the name as the mark of identity, but the purported evidence brought forth on a first person basis by the narration turns out to be self-contradictory.

The second paragraph begins with an oxymoron. A surname, Miklosich, without further clarification is given as the source of the next attribution to be contested. The 'much too famous page' in the narrator's text becomes a completely unknown and unknowable page. The dialectic between all or nothing remains a mainstay in the Borges repertoire.

The narrator-commentator now turns from the discussion of textual evidence to the rejection of unsubstantiated assertions linking the members of the sect first with the gypsies and secondly with the Jews. The syntactical structure of parallel comparisons is used:

A Gypsies are traders, coppersmiths, blacksmiths, and fortune tellers.

A^1 Gypsies constitute a certain physical type and speak, or used to speak, a secret language.

A^2 Gypsies are picturesque and inspire bad poets.

B The sectarians usually practise the liberal professions with success.

B^1 The sectarians are confused with the rest of men, and the proof lies in that they have not suffered persecutions.

B^2 Ballads, cheap illustrations, and foxtrots omit the sectarians.

By contrasting A, A^1, and A^2 with B, B^1, and B^2 the text refutes the simple coincidence of place; however, the argument is a sham since the commonplace acceptance of the first part of the contrasting pairs – gypsies – lulls the reader into accepting the second part – the sect – which is thus far empty of any significance since sectarians have as yet no identity, and without identity they cannot have attributes.

With the sole hiatus of three ellipsis marks the parallel argument is used for a second time to dispute the purported linkage of the sect with the Jews. Once again the first statement sets out to dismiss the assertion about the origin of the sect, but this time our commentator tires of the game rapidly and passes on to the general refutation of identity by association. Taken to its logical end, this argument creates an inversion between identity and non-identity. If the sectarians assimilate with everyone, they exist in name only as enunciated by our commentator.

The third paragraph, the shortest in the text, restates the non-identity of the sect: 'There is no human group in which members of the sect do not figure.' At this point the commentator has put before us only a name of dubious origin that purports to name a non-identifiable group.

The fourth paragraph, also the longest, is marked by a change in the formal structure. We first encounter a series of eliminations of all of the traditional attributes of a religious group until only one remains. The sole sign of identity of the sect is the secret.

The parodic mode leads us from one cul de sac to another. The statements have a similar syntactic structure; the proposition is not A but rather B, in which the A term is negative and the B term positive. The secret, we are told, is transmitted from generation to generation, but it is passed on not by mothers or priests but by the lowest individuals (slave, leper, or beggar). Before we can respond to the social significance of such practice, the category is dismissed as irrelevant. 'Also one child may indoctrinate another.' The transmission of the ritual has been reduced to children indoctrinating children.

But the most destructive term yet comes with the extreme reduction of a word without description: 'The act in itself is trivial, momentary and requires no description.'

HISTORICITY OF THE TEXT

The historical dimension of this text does not consist in following up the numerous historical and psuedo-historical clues that Borges has provided. We do that when we play the game of reading the conceptual labyrinth. What concerns us as the historical dimension is the meaning and value given to the concepts of faith, ritual, and instinct. The people of the custom or the secret or the sect of the Phoenix have only one thing in common: they possess a ritual that has become instinctive. There is no claim to faith throughout the text, and of course there is a complete absence of description of the rite itself. The absence of a specific rite makes it applicable to all religious rites. In a historical inquiry we recognize that in the second half of the twentieth century it is commonplace to accept that religious ritual has become instinctive to many and that this is so precisely because of the absence of faith. The historicity of the text moves the obvious syntactical play of oxymoron, contradiction, and parody into a much larger context, which is the distance between twentieth-century man and the *homo religiosus* of antiquity. The finest characterization of this unbridgeable distance has been made by Mircea Eliade in *The Sacred and the Profane*:

The non-religious man refuses transcendence, accepts the relativity of 'reality' and may even come to doubt the meaning of existence ... Modern non-religious man assumes a new existential situation; he regards himself solely as the subject and agent of history, and he refuses all appeal to transcendence. In other words, he accepts no model for humanity outside the human condition as it can be seen by the various historical situations. Man makes himself, and he only makes himself completely in proportion as he describes himself and the world. The sacred is the prime obstacle to his freedom. He will become himself only when he is totally demysticized. He will not be truly free until he has killed the last god. (202–3)

Our text omits all reference to belief on the part of sectarians; this omission is crucial for an understanding of the riddle strategy that confronts the reader, but it is also part of the historicity of Borges as a writer. Jaime Alazraki sums up the essential aspects of the historicity of Borges's writings:

The common denominator of all his fiction can be defined as a relativity which governs all things and which by being the result of a confrontation of opposites, takes on the appearance of a paradox and, at times, of an oxymoron: a traitor who is a hero (theme of the 'Traitor and the Hero'), a *Don Quixote* written in the 20th century identical to Cervantes' and at the same time immensely richer ('Pierre Menard, Author of the *Quixote*'), a library of unreadable books ('The Library of Babel'), a pursued pursuer ('Death and the Compass'), a divinity whom everyone looks for and does not find because everyone is the sought divinity ('The Approach to Al-Mu'tasim'), a minute that is a year ('The Secret Miracle'), a Judas who is Christ ('Three Versions of Judas'), a letter that contains the universe ('The Aleph'), a man who lives, but who is already dead ('The Dead Man'), a false story which is substantially true ('Emma Zunz'), a night that exhausts the life story of a man ('Biography of Tado Isidoro Cruz'). (*Jorge Luis Borges*, 45–6)

We can add to this list a ritual act of which, although there are no decent words to name it, it is understood that all words name it, or a secret that is sacred but is nevertheless somewhat ridiculous. Alazraki continues his summary: 'Although 'A' may exclude 'B,' Borges presents them together, co-existing to show that exclusion is deceitful because, while they reject and oppose each other, they also complement and need each other' (46). Thus it is that we can explain the use of contradiction in Borges's writing. It is not self-destructive but rather exists in a closed dichotomous relationship based on a change in perspective. In our text the perspective is the presence and absence of faith.

We have thus far considered both the semiotic and the semantic levels of Borges's text. The basis of semiotic inquiry is the analysis of the multi-dimensional make-up of the verbal sign when someone says or writes something for another to comprehend. The verbal sign in so far as it is language has syntactic structure as a part of the language system. In operation it also has syntagmatic and paradigmatic relationships which upon close scrutiny produce the mode of operation of the specific text. But the sign also means something and thus has a semantic relationship to the use of conceptual units and the creation of new ones, and this comes to be not within the word (sign) but in discourse. Thirdly, the sign as a part of a text participates in an intentional structure since it has been produced as purposeful utterance and is directed at an intentional recipient. Therefore the sign also participates in an intentional relationship that establishes the intersubjective basis for interpretation. Interpretation itself engages the text at the hermeneutic level. The three dimensions – semiotic, semantic, and intersubjective – are interconnected in a special way that we will emphasize at the end of this study.

APPROPRIATION: EXPLANATION AND UNDERSTANDING

I would now like to turn to the intentional strategy of the text, which provides the basis for the intersubjective study. There are three essential parts to the intentional strategy of this text. The first is the negative side of the argument, that is, the rejection of philological evidence with regard to the origin of the sect or its name, the rejection of the facile attempts at identity of the sect through analogy first with the gypsies and then with the Jews.

Secondly, there is the positive argument that reaffirms the existence of the sect, but reduces its identity to one term – the Secret – which is always written in upper case; the Secret is subsequently further reduced to the rite of the sect.

The third and most important part of the intentional strategy is the proposition posed by the riddle created by the negative and positive arguments. The fourth paragraph is given over entirely to the presentation of the riddle. Let us review it. The sole basis of identity for the sect of the Phoenix is the Secret, which is the rite. The riddle is given in four triads: A / the mystagogues are 1 / a slave, 2 / a leper, or 3 / a beggar, but a child can be substituted for these three; B / there are specific materials used in the rite –1 / cork, 2 / wax, or 3 / gum arabic, but once again mud may be substituted for these; C / the most propitious places for the performance of the rite are 1 / certain ruins, 2 / a cellar, or 3 / an entrance hall, and this time there is no substitution, but there is a specific elimination – there are no temples; and D / the act itself is 1 / trivial, 2 / momentary, and 3 / requires no description.

The riddle can be paraphrased as a series of paradoxical statements that underline the incompatibility of the triads. A child using mud in an entrance-way in a trivial and momentary manner comprises the sacred rite of the Secret. The paradox mounts up, for the rite is sacred but it is also ridiculous; there are no words to express it, but all words allude to it; those who do not perform the rite are faithful believers; others despise them for not performing the rite, but they despise themselves even more; those who deliberately renounce the rite attain direct contact with the divinity, and finally, the practice of the rite is so widespread that it is now said to have become instinctive. The reader is plunged into the labyrinth of the riddle and must struggle to find his way out.

The intentional strategy has trapped the reader and the way out is to reconsider whether all the terms have the significance that we grant them as a matter of course in our reading. It is at this point that we must re-read the following lines from the fourth paragraph: 'Once, in addition to the Secret, there was a legend (and perhaps a cosmogonic myth), but the shallow men of the Phoenix have forgotten it and now only retain the obscure tradition of a punishment. Of a punishment, of a pact or of a privilege, for the versions differ and scarcely allow us to glimpse the verdict of a God who granted eternity to a lineage if its members, generation after generation, would perform a rite.'

CRITICAL INTERPRETATION

The riddle strategy has exploited the problem-solving capacities of the reader. The more knowledgeable the reader is about the history of religion, the more he will be induced to go deeper into the labyrinth, for the riddle defies all historical or rational solutions because the Secret is a denotative and not a connotative term. As the above-cited paragraph indicates, there is no belief, no faith; the ritual is an empty gesture. The only *true* statement that is possible about the Secret is that it has six letters, is written in upper case, and has a lexical definition as 'something not to be told.' Therefore, if it were told, the telling would violate its definition and would contradict itself not in a dichotomous relationship of opposition but in an absolute manner of complete elimination. The only secret that can truly qualify as the Secret is the one that can never be told because it is pure denotation with no connotation. Therefore all attributes of identity that plague the reader serve to establish the presence that sets off the absence, or, in other words, the triads of attributes are the circumference that denotes the hole that is the instinctive gesture.

The hermeneutic reflection on the riddle of 'The Sect of the Phoenix' opens up the consideration of other anomalies, such as the person who makes the sign of the cross out of instinct, not as a practice of faith, or the act of rapping the knuckles on wood when bad fortune is mentioned, or asking 'How are you' without awaiting or even acknowledging a response.

A perceptive logician will argue that inference, while necessary to sustain the validity of arguments based on experience, is itself not capable of being proved by experience, and yet it is unhesitatingly believed by everyone because it 'makes sense,' at least in its concrete applications, and is usually taken as the primary assumption of demonstration. Therefore our logician can argue that whatever we present as a hermeneutic commentary on a literary text is in fact a series of inferences drawn from our experience of reading the text, but that the very process of drawing inferences cannot be proven. The flaw in this form of reasoning is the assumption that the aim of hermeneutic commentary is to isolate a definitive truth about the text under scrutiny. As I have argued before in this book, there are alternative aims to criticism, and the one that is the subject of this study is the aim of sharing and participating in the experience of others. I have not imposed closure on this text through the hermeneutic interpretation, for the inferences I have drawn from the reading experience buttressed by formal analysis and historical inquiry are proposed as a shared meaning clearly intended to be temporary and provocative.

8

Concluding Assessment of Critical Commentaries

Now that the commentary has been completed, what is it that I purport to have achieved by writing it? What possible difference will it make to readers of Paz and Borges? Do I, in fact, contribute anything to that purported community of scholars to whom I have alluded, and what is the essence of this temporary truth I have tried to capture? These are some of the many questions that my critical work elicits when it is set in the context of the theory of criticism I have presented. There will also be the response of those readers who will want to rescue a sense of lost innocence and proclaim that the commentary is valid by itself and stands by itself without all of the heavy-handed theorizing that I have presented.

I shall begin my response to these questions and admonitions in reverse order. First, it is quite proper and correct for my criticism to stand by itself and not as the illustration of theory, for it would not be criticism if it were merely a point-by-point expansion of more abstract arguments. In criticism the focus must be on the text from the point of view of the scholarly community to which both my readers and I belong. Theory is not part of criticism; it is metacriticism. It is the concern of a practitioner for his craft.

Where is the truth in my commentary? The truth of literature is the resulting redescription of the world of action that the reading of the text has thrust upon me. In order to make the possible world of the text, I must in fact rediscover the world. As long as the remaking of my world remains a private sense of being, there can be no truth-claim by me as a reader. It is only when I seek to share the remaking of the world with others that there is a question of truth. The concept of truth in both commentaries stands as an intentional act by myself, as commentator, to communicate my remaking of the world through the text as an ontologically possible world. Therefore, the truth of redescription does not stand in the text, nor does it impose closure on the text, but rather it stands alongside the text, among numerous other possible worlds, in a tradition of learned response.

Does the community of scholars truly exist in the present, and is there a viable past? Although there are, undoubtedly, a few readers who attempt to use literary criticism as a surrogate for the literary text, the majority of those who read literary criticism are literary critics and students of literary criticism who have already fairly well-defined perimeters around the literary text in question and who thus, in the best of cases, are much more likely to engage in a productive conflict with the criticism they are reading and, in the worst of cases, will simply reject it as inappropriate for debate. The engagement of minds on the meaning of literature is the unifying mark of the community. The traditional practice of footnotes or endnotes used in literary scholarship is, in fact, nothing other than a sub-text to the commentary one that engages in the undertaking as many other critics as are known to the critic, but even when this subtext is absent, the engagement of the community is a practical necessity, which book publishers fully understand. The engagement with the critics of the past is the mark of scholarship and distinguishes the craftsman from the mere apprentice.

What difference will these commentaries make to readers of Paz and Borges? Although I have already partially responded to this question, it bears fuller discussion. I begin with the assumption that my interpretation of the text is not acceptable, at least in part, to my readers; further, I also do not expect that they should change their views to conform to mine, but what I fully expect is that they will be able to understand why and how I have come to my interpretation and that the interpretation I offer will be accepted as possible for the text in question. The enrichment that will be the dividend of my readers comes about because of the debate they will have with me, issuing from the clash and conflict that ensues from their previous notions of the text and the ones that I have inserted into the discussion. Do I assume too much? I think not. I am counting on previous knowledge of the text and a healthy sense of opposition to my intrusion into the comfortable world that my readers have worked out for themselves and into which they have assimilated the text. Perhaps the greatest dividend of all is the liberation of the text from the pre-ordained universe of literary histories.

I now come to my initial question, which revolves around the aims of literary criticism. My aims, which are common to all critics, are to enrich the tradition by respecting the text's integrity and my colleagues' essential differences.

APPENDIX

La secta del Fénix / The Sect of the Phoenix

Quienes escriben que la secta del Fénix tuvo su origen en Heliópolis, y la derivan de la restauración religiosa que sucedió a la muerte del reformador Amenophis IV, alegan textos de Heródoto, de Tácito y de los monumentos egipcios, pero ignoran, o quieren ignorar, que la denominación por el Fénix no es anterior a Hrabano Mauro y que las fuentes más antiguas (las *Saturnales* o Flavio Josefo, digamos) sólo hablan de la Gente de la Costumbre o de la Gente del Secreto. Ya Gregorovius observó, en los conventículos de Ferrara, que la mención del Fénix era rarísima en el lenguaje oral; en Ginebra he tratado con artesanos que no me comprendieron cuando inquirí si eran hombres del Fénix, pero que admitieron, acto continuo, ser hombres del Secreto. Si no me engaño, igual cosa acontece con los budistas; el nombre por el cual los conoce el mundo no es el que ellos pronuncian.

Miklosich, en una página demasiado famosa, ha equiparado los sectarios del Fénix a los gitanos. En Chile y en Hungría hay gitanos y también hay sectarios; fuera de esa especie de ubicuidad, muy poco tienen en común unos y otros. Los gitanos son chalanes, caldereros, herreros y decidores de la buenaventura; los sectarios suelen ejercer felizmente las profesiones liberales. Los gitanos configuran un tipo físico y hablan, o hablaban, un idioma secreto; los sectarios se confunden con los demás y la prueba es que no han sufrido persecuciones. Los gitanos son pintorescos e inspiran a los malos poetas; los romances, los cromos y los boleros omiten a los sectarios … Martín Buber declara que los judíos son esencialmente patéticos; no todos los sectarios lo son y algunos abominan del patetismo; esta pública, y notoria verdad basta para refutar el error vulgar (absurdamente defendido por Urmann) que ve en el Fénix una derivación de Israel. La gente más o menos discurre así: Urmann era un hombre sensible;

Urmann era judío; Urmann frecuentó a los sectarios en la judería de Praga; la afinidad que Urmann sintió prueba un hecho real. Sinceramente, no puedo convenir con ese dictamen. Que los sectarios en un medio judío se parezcan a los judíos no prueba nada; lo innegable es que se parecen, como el infinito Shakespeare de Hazlitt, a todos los hombres del mundo. Son todo para todos, como el Apóstol; días pasados el doctor Juan Francisco Amaro, de Paysandu, ponderó la facilidad con que se acriollaban.

He dicho que la historia de la secta no registra persecuciones. Ello es verdad, pero como no hay grupo humano en que no figuren partidarios del Fénix, también es cierto que no hay persecución o rigor que éstos no hayan sufrido y ejecutado. En las guerras occidentales y en las remotas guerras del Asia han vertido su sangre secularmente, bajo banderas enemigas; de muy poco les vale identificarse con todas las naciones del orbe.

Sin un libro sagrado que los congregue como la Escritura a Israel, sin una memoria común, sin esa otra memoria que es un idioma, desparramados por la faz de la tierra, diversos de color y de rasgos, una sola cosa – el Secreto – los une y los unirá hasta el fin de los días. Alguna vez, además del Secreto hubo una leyenda (y quizá un mito cosmogónico), pero los superficiales hombres del Fénix la han olvidado y hoy sólo guardan la oscura tradición de un castigo. De un castigo, de un pacto o de un privilegio, porque las versiones difieren y apenas dejan entrever el fallo de un Dios que asegura a una estirpe la eternidad, si sus hombres, generación tras generación, ejecutan un rito. He compulsado los informes de los viajeros, he conversado con patriarcas y teólogos; puedo dar fe de que el cumplimiento del rito es la única práctica religiosa que observan los sectarios. El rito constituye el Secreto. Este, como ya indiqué, se trasmite de generación en generación, pero el uso no quiere que las madres lo enseñen a los hijos, ni tampoco los sacerdotes; la iniciación en el misterio es tarea de los individuos más bajos. Un esclavo, un leproso o un pordiosero hacen de mistagogos. También un niño puede adoctrinar a otro niño. El acto en sí es trivial, momentáneo y no requiere descripción. Los materiales son el corcho, la cera o la goma arábiga. (En la liturgia se habla de légamo; éste suele usarse también.) No hay templos dedicados especialmente a la celebración de este culto, pero una ruina, un sótano o un zaguán se juzgan lugares propicios. El Secreto es sagrado pero no deja de ser un poco ridículo; su ejercicio es furtivo y aun clandestino y los adeptos no hablan de él. No hay palabras decentes para nombrarlo, pero se entiende que todas las palabras lo nombran o, mejor dicho, que inevitablemente lo aluden, y así, en el diálogo yo he dicho una cosa cualquiera y los adeptos han sonreído o se han puesto incómodos, porque sintieron que yo había tocado el Secreto. En las literaturas germánicas hay poemas escritos por sectarios, cuyo sujeto nominal es el mar o el crepúsculo de la noche; son, de algún modo, símbolos del Secreto, oigo repetir. *Orbis terrarum est speculum Ludi* reza un adagio apócrifo que Du Cange registró en su Glosario. Una suerte de horror sagrado impide a algunos fieles la ejecución del simplísimo rito; los otros los desprecían, pero ellos se desprecian aun más. Gozan de mucho crédito, en cambio, quienes deliberadamente renuncian a la Costumbre y logran un comercio directo con la divinidad; éstos, para manifestar ese comercio, lo hacen con figuras de la liturgia y así. John of the Rood escribió:

Sepan los Nueve Firmamentos que el Dios
Es deleitable como el Corcho y el Cieno.

He merecido en tres continentes la amistad de muchos devotos del Fénix; me consta que el secreto, al principio, les pareció baladí, penoso, vulgar y (lo que aun es más extraño) increíble. No se avenían a admitir que sus padres se hubieran rebajado a tales manejos. Lo raro es que el Secreto no se haya perdido hace tiempo; a despecho de las vicisitudes del orbe, a despecho de las guerras y de los éxodos, llega, tremendamente, a todos los fieles. Alguien no ha vacilado en afirmar que ya es instintivo.

Those who write that the sect of the Phoenix had its origin in Heliopolis and derive it from the religious restoration following upon the death of the reformer Amenophis IV, cite texts from Herodotus, Tacitus and the monuments of Egypt, but they ignore, or prefer to ignore, that the designation 'Phoenix' does not date before Hrabanus Maurus and that the oldest sources (the *Saturnales* of Flavius Josephus, let us say) speak only of the People of the Custom or of the People of the Secret. Gregorovius has already observed, in the conventicles of Ferrara, that mention of the Phoenix was very rare in oral speech; in Geneva I have known artisans who did not understand me when I inquired if they were men of the Phoenix, but who immediately admitted being men of the Secret. If I am not deceived, the same is true of the Buddhists; the name by which the world knows them is not the one they themselves utter.

Miklosich, in a page much too famous, has compared the sectarians of the Phoenix with the gypsies. In Chile and in Hungary there are gypsies and there are also sectarians; aside from this sort of ubiquity, one and the other have very little in common. The gypsies are traders, copper-smiths, blacksmiths and fortunetellers; the sectarians usually practice the liberal professions with success. The gypsies constitute a certain physical type and speak, or used to speak, a secret language; the sectarians are confused with the rest of men and the proof lies in that they have not suffered persecutions. The gypsies are picturesque and inspire bad poets; ballads, cheap illustrations and foxtrots omit the sectarians ... Martin Buber declares that the Jews are essentially pathetic; not all sectarians are and some deplore the pathetic; this public and notorious truth is sufficient to refute the common error (absurdly defended by Urmann) which sees the Phoenix as a derivation of Israel. People more or less reason in this manner: Urmann was a sensitive man; Urmann was a Jew; Urmann came in frequent contact with the sectarians in the ghetto of Prague; the affinity Urmann sensed proves the reality of the fact. In all sincerity, I cannot concur with this dictum. That sectarians in a Jewish environment should resemble the Jews proves nothing; the undeniable fact is that, like Hazlitt's infinite Shakespeare, they resemble all the men in the world. They are everything for everyone, like the Apostle; several days ago, Dr Juan Francisco Amaro, of Paysandú, admired the facility with which they assimilated Creole ways.

I have said that the history of the sect records no persecutions. This is true, but since there is no human group in which members of the sect do not figure, it is also true that there is no persecution or rigor they have not suffered and perpetrated. In the Occidental wars and in the remote wars of Asia they have shed their blood secularly, under opposing banners; it avails them very little to identify themselves with all the nations of the world.

Without a sacred book to join them as the scriptures do for Israel, without a common memory, without that other memory which is a language, scattered over the face of the earth, diverse in color and features, one thing alone – the Secret – unites them and will unite them until the end of time. Once, in addition to the Secret, there was a legend (and perhaps a cosmogonic myth), but the shallow men of the Phoenix have forgotten it and now only retain the obscure tradition of a punishment. Of a punishment, of a pact or of a privilege, for the versions differ and scarcely allow us to glimpse the verdict of a God who granted eternity to a lineage if its members, generation after generation, would perform a rite. I have collated accounts by travelers, I have conversed with patriarchs and theologians; I can testify that fulfillment of the rite is the only religious practice observed by the sectarians. The rite constitutes the Secret. This Secret, as I have already indicated, is transmitted from generation to generation, but good usage prefers that mothers should not teach it to their children, nor that priests should; initiation into the mystery is the task of the lowest individuals. A slave, a leper or a beggar serve as mystagogues. Also one child may indoctrinate another. The act in itself is trivial, momentary and requires no description. The materials are cork, wax or gum arabic. (In the liturgy, mud is mentioned; this is often used as well.) There are no temples especially dedicated to the celebration of this cult, but certain ruins, a cellar or an entrance hall are considered propitious places. The Secret is sacred but is always somewhat ridiculous; its performance is furtive and even clandestine and the adept do not speak of it. There are no decent words to name it, but it is understood that all words name it or, rather, inevitably allude to it, and thus, in a conversation I say something or other and the adept smile or become uncomfortable, for they realize I have touched upon the Secret. In Germanic literatures there are poems written by sectarians whose nominal subject is the sea or the twilight of evening; they are, in some way, symbols of the Secret, I hear it said repeatedly. *Orbis terrarum est speculum Ludi* reads an apocryphal adage recorded by Du Cange in his Glossary. A kind of sacred horror prevents some faithful believers from performing this very simple rite; the others despise them, but they despise themselves even more. Considerable credit is enjoyed, however, by those who deliberately renounce the custom and attain direct contact with the divinity; these sectarians, in order to express this contact, do so with figures taken from the liturgy and thus John of the Rood wrote:

May the Seven Firmaments know that God
Is as delectable as the Cork and the Slime.

I have attained on three continents the friendship of many devotés of the Phoenix; I know that the Secret, at first, seemed to them banal, embarrassing, vulgar and (what is even stranger) incredible. They could not bring themselves to admit their parents had stooped to such manipulations. What is odd is that the Secret was not lost long ago; in spite of the vicissitudes of the Universe, in spite of wars and exoduses, it reaches, awesomely, all the faithful. Someone has not hesitated to affirm that it is now instinctive.

Notes

1 See R. Cardona's review of *Shadows in the Cave*, in *Hispanic Review* (Winter 1985).

CHAPTER ONE: RELATIONAL THEORY

1 Throughout these comments I use the Spanish translation of the complete works of Vives by Lorenzo Riber because of the accuracy of the edition. I have also read the English translation of *Against the Pseudodialecticians* by Rita Guerlac, but I do not cite from it. All English translations from Spanish are mine unless otherwise noted in the text.

2 The remarkable achievement of Giambattista Vico has long since been recognized and acknowledged by Benedetto Croce, *La filosofia di Giambattista Vico* (1947), and by Croce's English translator, the British philosopher R.G. Collingwood, *The Philosophy of Giambattista Vico* (1913). I am of course greatly indebted to Professor Max H. Fisch for his introduction to the English translation of *La scienza nuova* and to the excellent translation that he and Thomas Goddard Bergin have provided for us in English. All quotations are from the 1968 English translation.

3 See *The New Science*, 112, sec. 367: 'We shall show clearly and distinctly how the founders of gentile humanity by means of their natural theology (or metaphysics) imagined the gods; how by means of their logic they invented languages; by morals created heroes; by economics, founded families, and by politics, cities; by their physics, established the beginnings of things as all divine; by the particular physics of man, in a certain sense created themselves.' Max Fisch comments in the introduction, xliv:

The rationalistic theory assumed that the institutions of society were made by 'men,' in the sense of human beings who were already fully human, in whom the humanity of Vico's 'age of men' was already fully developed. What Vico wanted to assert was that the first steps in the building of the 'world of nations' were taken by creatures who were still beasts, and that humanity itself was created by the very same process by which institutions were created. Humanity is not a presupposition, but a consequence, an effect, a product of institution building [c6,J2]. Vico indeed carries this so far as to assert that it was not only in respect of mind or spirit, but in respect of body or 'corporature,' also, that these creatures-not-yet-human made themselves human [520, 692].

This cryptic comment has been taken up in depth by André Missenard, *A la recherche de l'homme*, trans. Blochman, *In Search of Man*: 'Thought is the slave of our means of expression ... The intellectual capital of a nation is invested in its language' (267).

4 *The New Science*, 120, Sec. 384: 'All that has been so far said here upsets all the theories of the origin of poetry from Plato and Aristotle down to Patrizzi, Scaliger, and Castelvetro [807]. For it has been shown that it was deficiency of human reasoning power that gave rise to poetry so sublime that the philosophies which came afterward, the arts of poetry and of criticism, have produced none equal or better, and have even prevented its production.' Robert Caponigri, *Time and Idea: The Theory of History in Giambattista Vico*, comments: 'The heart of the Vichian conception of poetry, and his great discovery, is its necessity ... Early documents are poetic in form, even in the most external sense of the term, because the consciousness of early man was itself intimately and constitutively poetic. Poetry consequently becomes the defining term of the inner quality of the first-time form moment, which [Vico] has to this point characterized as spontaneous and which he has further analysed into the sense-phantasy complex. And poetic becomes the adjective by which he designates and describes the whole pre-reflective life of man' (165–6).

5 See *The New Science*, 65–6, sec. 147–59.

6 The philosophy of language of Wilhelm von Humboldt has finally come into its time. In our age of post-structuralist theory it would do every theorist well to read the key passages of his philosophy of language, written for the most part in his later years; an excellent selection and translation of these writings is contained in Marianne Cowan's *Anthology of the Writings of Wilhelm von Humboldt: Humanist Without Portfolio*; the pertinent chapter is 'Man's Intrinsic Humanity: His Language,' 235–98. I cite from 235ff:

All understanding is also a misunderstanding.

No one when he uses a word has in mind exactly the same thing that another has, and the difference, however tiny, sends its tremors throughout language, if one may compare language with the most volatile element. With each thought, each feeling, this difference returns, thanks to the element of unvarying identity in individuality, and finally forms a mass of elements which singly went unnoticed. All understanding, therefore, is always at the same time a misunderstanding – this being a truth which it is most useful to know in practical life – and all agreement of feelings and thoughts is at the same time a means for growing apart (*Werke* v, 396).

Language everywhere mediates, first between infinite and finite nature, then between one individual and another. Simultaneously and through the same act it makes union possible and itself originates from it. The whole of its nature never lies in singularity but must always simultaneously be guessed or intuited from otherness (*Werke* III, 296–7).

Every language sets certain limits to the spirit of those who speak it; it assumes a certain direction and, by doing so, excludes others (*Werke* VII, 621).

7 The significance and historical importance of Saussure's theory of language cannot be overestimated. It was a revolutionary theory and still remains one of the foundations of present-day semiotics. There are, however, a number of aspects of the *Cours de linguistique générale* that continue to isolate abstractions of literary texts as permanent models for these texts, and it is this part of Saussure's legacy that I reject. Following Benveniste I consider the sign the basic unit of semiotics and the sentence the unit of semantics. Each of these belongs to different orders of language use, and they therefore have different areas of operation and generate different restricted meanings. The system of signs is but one of the aspects of language and does not represent the total phenomenon.

Paul Ricoeur takes up the analysis of Saussure's theory of language in *The Rule of Metaphor* (120–32), wherein he examines the narrowness of Saussure's various dichotomies – for example, signifier-signified.

8 Rorty, *Philosophy and The Mirror of Nature*, 367. The context in which Rorty is writing is a contrastive review of what he terms 'Systematic Philosophy and Edifying Philosophy,' wherein he proposes: 'A "mainstream" Western philosopher typically says: Now that such-and-such a line of inquiry has had such a stunning success, let us reshape all inquiry, and all of culture, on

its model, thereby permitting objectivity and rationality to prevail in areas previously obscured by convention, superstition, and the lack of a proper epistemological understanding of man's ability accurately to represent nature.' Rorty has no argument from me with regard to what he calls systematic and edifying philosophers. What is not acceptable is his view that 'the hermeneutic point of view [is one] from which the acquisition of truth dwindles in importance' (365). What he has not recognized is that there can be more than the absolute truth of categories in the quest of the hermeneutic philosopher such as Gadamer and Ricoeur.

9 There have been two editions of the Spanish translation, 1912 and 1926; all editions subsequent to 1926 have merely been reprintings. The edition used here is Croce, *Estética como ciencia de la expresión y linguistica general* (1926). The prologue by Unamuno has also been included in his *Obras Completas*, vol. 8, 986–1000.

10 For further consideration of this fundamental aspect of Unamuno's philosophy see my *Death in the Literature of Unamuno*, 6–15, and also my prologue to *An Unamuno Source Book*.

11 The relationship between Unamuno and Miró has been examined in detail by a number of critics, the foremost study being that of Roberta Johnson, 'The Genesis of Gabriel Miro's Ideas about Being and Language: The Barcelona Period 1914–1920.'

12 The Norton lectures of 1958 were published in English with the title *Language and Poetry*, trans. *Lenguaje y poesía: algunos casos Españoles*. I quote from the chapter on Miró, 'Lenguaje suficiente: Gabriel Miró,' 185–232: 'Miró dice más: el acto contemplativo se realiza del todo gracias al acto verbal. Entonces se cumple el ciclo de la experiencia. Hasta que no "se pronuncia" esa experiencia no acaba de vivirse' (186). Miro says more: the act of contemplation is realized only owing to the verbal act that preceded it. It is only then that the cycle of experience is completed. It is not until the experience is pronounced that it is fully lived.

Cf Unamuno, *Obras Completas*, vol. 4, 437–40 (cited and commented upon in *Shadows in the Cave*, 5): 'Expresar algo es enterarse de ello, ni nadie puede saber si sabe algo hasta que no lo ha expresado'; 'To express something is to understand it; nobody can be sure of knowing anything until he has expressed it.' My comment on this passage is appropriate in the present context: 'I know the world through my experience and I am aware of experience because I organize and form it and I can organize the world because I express myself.'

13 Octavio Paz can only be compared to Paul Valéry and T.S. Eliot as a poet whose reflective commentary on poetic language stands irrespective of

his achievements as a poet. I cite one brief passage from *Corriente Alterna*:

> digo que en poesía el sentido es inseparable de la palabra, es palabra, en tanto que en el discurso ordinario, así sea el del místico, el sentido es aquello que denotan las palabras y que está más allá del lenguaje. La experiencia del poeta es ante todo verbal; o sí se quiere: toda experiencia, en poesía, adquiere inmediatamente una tonalidad verbal. (5)

> I say that in poetry meaning is inseparable from the words, it is the words themselves; in contrast, in ordinary discourse, including mystical works, meaning is that which the words denote and which stands beyond language. The poet's experience is above all verbal,or if one prefers: all experience in poetry immediately acquires verbal tonality.

Vico, Croce, and Unamuno would merely add that that which stands beyond language is knowable only through language and has no distinctive characteristics unless it is acknowledged through language. As matter and energy it may be present, but as man's perception of matter and energy it must be available through language. The poet is thus the master world-maker in the community.

14 Edward Sapir's work is not generally known by literary critics because of the specific nature of his research and its publication in the journals of the social sciences. There is, however, a deep kinship in his work with the relational theory of interpretation that I have been sketching in this chapter. In the selected essays published under the title *Culture, Language and Personality* he vigorously attacks the abstractions of the anthropologist as pseudo-objectivity: 'their integrations into suggested structures are uniformly fallacious and unreal' (200). He further develops the concept that culture might be something constituted by individual human beings as a 'world of meanings' – that is to say that the language of participation of the individual with the group was a shared world-view.

15 *Language, Culture and Personality*, 162. The key issue here and throughout these essays is the rejection of the purported objective real world of anthropologists: 'Human beings do not live in the objective world alone, nor alone in the world of social activity as ordinarily understood, but are very much at the mercy of the particular language which has become the medium of expression for their society.'

16 Lévi-Strauss's kinship with the Humboldt-Sapir-Whorf concept of man as world-maker is fully documented and does not require detailed attention

on my part. There are, however, significant differences between the relational development I have been examining and the structuralism of Lévi-Strauss. Let me begin with a quotation from *La Pensée sauvage* (*The Savage Mind*): 'This reciprocity of perspectives, in which man and the world mirror each other and which seems to us the only possible explanation of the properties and capacities of the savage mind, we thus find transposed to the plane of mechanized civilization ... The beings confront each other face to face as subjects and objects at the same time; and in the code they employ, a simple variation in the distance separating them has the force of a silent adjuration' (222). Language being the primary code of world-making, it follows that the Jakobson–Lévi-Strauss concept of language is the focal point of our inquiry into the development of the relational idea. The idea that language is a closed system of signs and that within this system each element refers to other elements in the system clearly separates structuralism from the relational concept of Vico. To Lévi-Strauss language cannot refer to anything outside of itself since it is a self-constituted world.

It is instructive to note that Lévi-Strauss faulted B.L. Whorf's studies for lacking an integrating theory, that is, a concept of closed system; see *Anthropologie Structurale*, trans. *Structural Anthropology*, 85. The critique of Lévi-Strauss by Edmund Leach, *Lévi-Strauss*, is very useful, especially chapter 5, 'Words and Things.' For further study of Whorf see George Steiner, *After Babel*, 88–94.

17 Although the work of Jean Piaget is tangential to the main discussion of this chapter, I have given some attention to his views because of his efforts in pursuing interdisciplinary research on man's way of perceiving and his careful set of definitions of structuralism. In *Le structuralisme*, trans. *Structuralism*, 5–16, he proposes three fundamental conditions for there to be a structure: wholeness, capacity to transform materials within, and self-regulation. *Wholeness* is primarily the means of attaining internal coherence. A structure is not a composite or an aggregate. The constituent parts of a structure have no independent existence. *Transformation*: a structure is conceived by Piaget as a dynamic process whereby it continually adds new elements through its transformational procedures. *Self-regulation*: this is one of the most important of Piaget's concepts. He holds that the structure must make no appeal beyond itself in order to radiate its transformational procedures. In our terms this means that the structure is understood as a closed system that can be changed.

18 Merleau-Ponty gave 'Le Primat de la perception' as a lecture on 23 November 1946 to the Société Française de Philosophie; it was subsequently published in the *Bulletin de la Société Française de Philosophie* 41, no 4: 119–153, and

translated by James M. Edie and published in *The Primacy of Perception*, 12–42. *Phénoménologie de la perception* has been translated by Colin Smith and published as *Phenomenology of Perception*. I have used two commentaries on Merleau-Ponty's relation to structuralism: Lanigan, *Speaking and Semiology*, 75–96, and Mallin, *Merleau-Ponty's Philosophy*, 31–51. Bannan, *The Philosophy of Merleau-Ponty*, has been especially useful in my first encounter with Merleau-Ponty's writings in 1968–69 and the subsequent development of the idea of a tradition of relational criticism; see especially 'Cogito, Time, and Freedom,' 115–138, and 'The Primacy of Perception and the Problem of Truth,' 141–67.

19 There are a number of valuable anthologies of Russian formalist critics. One of the first was Victor Erlich, *Russian Formalism: History-Doctrine* (1955). This book contains some important information on the historical background to the Moscow group. The anthology edited by Lee Lemon and Marion Reis, *Russian Formalist Criticism: Four Essays*, serves as a complement to Erlich's first book, since it makes available full essay studies by Shklovskij, Tomashevskij, and Eichenbaum. The book edited by Ladislav Matejka and Krystyna Pomorska, *Readings in Russian Poetics: Formalist and Structural Views*, contains an excellent selection of key critics with a clear emphasis on theory. The second anthology edited by Victor Erlich, *Twentieth-Century Russian Literary Criticism*, offers a concerted presentation of criticism. Jameson, *The Prison-House of Language: A Critical Account of Structuralism and Russian Formalism*, has served me as a critical review of Russian formalist theory.

20 I am indebted to my colleague Linda Hutcheon, whose clear analysis of the *Tel Quel* group has served me well in the present context; see *Narcissistic Narrative*, 125–30. The basic source for this discussion is *Tel Quel: Théorie d'ensemble*.

21 See my *Shadows in the Cave*, 3–14.

22 In these remarks on Barthes I am indebted to Terence Hawkes's lucid book *Structuralism and Semiotics*, 106–22. The sources from Barthes are *Le Degré zéro de l'écriture*, trans. *Writing Degree Zero*; *Eléments de sémiologie*, trans. *Elements of Semiology*, and finally his most extensive theoretical book, *S/Z*.

23 Iser, *The Implied Reader*, 274. I also wish to acknowledge Professor Iser's article 'Narrative Strategies as a Means of Communication,' in Valdés and Miller, eds., *Interpretation of Narrative*, 100–17, and *The Act of Reading*, which have been a major influence in the development of my theoretical thinking.

24 See Jauss, 'Theses on the Transition from the Aesthetics of Literary Works to a Theory of Aesthetic Experience,' in Valdés and Miller, eds., *Interpretation of Narrative*, 137–47.

CHAPTER TWO: THE ONTOLOGICAL STATUS OF THE LITERARY TEXT

1 The most notable writer to pursue this route is Stanley Fish, whose articles have been at the forefront of theoretical discussions for more than a decade. See 'How to recognize a poem when you see one,' in *Is There a Text in This Class?* 322–37.
2 I have profited greatly from my study of Eli Hirsch's excellent book *The Concept of Identity*. I am especially indebted to chapter 8, 'A Sense of Unity,' where he states: 'My argument against the empiricist position consisted in maintaining that there is nothing about the world which could have taught us to adopt our ordinary criteria of unity, had we started out without these criteria' (262).
3 I would like to acknowledge the work of Alfred Schutz as the basis of much of my thinking on communication and the social group. See *Der sinnhafte Aufbau der sozialen Welt*, trans. *The Phenomenology of the Social World*, especially 'The Meaning-Context of Communication,' 129–32.
4 Cf Paul Ricoeur: 'What do we understand by the referential relation or referential function? In addressing himself to another speaker, the subject of discourse says something about something; that about which he speaks is the referent of his discourse ... All discourse is, to some extent, thereby reconnected to the world. For if we did not speak of the world, of what should we speak? ... As we shall see, the text is not without reference; the task of reading, *qua* interpretation, will be precisely to fulfill the reference' ('What is a Text,' in *Hermeneutics and the Human Sciences*, 147–8).
5 See Iser, *The Act of Reading*. He writes: 'there are three types of "contemporary" reader – the one real and historical, drawn from existing documents, and the other two hypothetical: the first constructed from social and historical knowledge of the time, and the second extrapolated from the reader's role laid down in the text' (28).
6 One of the ironic twists of contemporary theory is that the concept of a super-reader or fixed norm of reading is little more than an objectification of the critic's own reading experience. On this issue see Iser, *The Act of Reading*, and Jauss, 'Theses on the Transition from the Aesthetics of Literary Works to a Theory of Aesthetic Experience,' in Valdés and Miller, eds., *Interpretation of Narrative*, 137–47: 'Whoever reduces the role of the implied reader to the behaviour of an explicit reader, whoever writes exclusively in the language of a specific stratum, can only produce cookbooks, catechisms, party speeches, travel brochures, and similar documents' (143).
7 Richard Rorty in his recent book, *Philosophy and the Mirror of Nature*, 361, sums up the argument: 'objectivity should be seen as conformity to the

norms of justification (for assertions and for actions) we find about us. Such
conformity becomes dubious and self-deceptive only when seen as something more than this – namely, as a way of obtaining access to something
which grounds current practices of justification in something else. Such a
ground is thought to need no justification, because it has become so clearly
and distinctly perceived as to count as a philosophical foundation. This is
self-deceptive not simply because of the general absurdity of ultimate justi-
fications reposing upon the unjustifiable, but because of the more concrete
absurdity of thinking that the vocabulary used by present science, morality or
whatever has some privileged attachment to reality which makes it *more*
than just a further set of descriptions.'

8 See my introduction to *An Unamuno Source Book,* xxi, n 15.

9 For a fuller understanding of Martínez Bonati's thought see his recent *Fictive
Discourse and the Structures of Literature* and his essay 'Hermeneutic Criticism and the Description of Form,' in Valdés and Miller, eds., *Interpretation of
Narrative,* 78–99, as well as his major statement on the question of identity, in Valdés and Miller, eds., *Identity of the Literary Text,* 231–45.

10 The deconstruction position is of course derived from Jacques Derrida's
theory of polysemy, in which he maintains that the semantic operation we call
deconstruction is a continuous mode of play with the text by the reader,
and its major aim is to destroy the illusory notion of a fixed textual meaning.
Every meaning that is presumed by the commentator to stand is shown to
be no more than a play between simulation and dissimulation. The true nature of every text therefore is to be in a state of flux as long as it is engaged
by the reader; it is reduced to a mere trace when the engagement is over
because the text has no determinate essence. Derrida apparently endorses
the following passage he cites from Rousseau's *Emile*: 'The dreams of a bad
night are given to us as philosophy. You will say I too am a dreamer; I
admit it, but I do what others fail to do, I give my dreams as dreams, and leave
the reader to discover whether there is anything in them which may prove
useful to those who are awake' (*Of Grammatology,* 316).

11 The author of a text is thus a historical fact and has significance within an
effective history of composition for the text in question. This position
stated briefly here is derived from Hans Georg Gadamer's major study
Wahrheit und Methode, trans. *Truth and Method.* I cite a key passage: 'The
naïveté of so-called historicism consists in the fact that it does not undertake this reflection, and in trusting to its own methodological approach for-
gets its own historicality ... True historical thinking must take account of
its own historicality. Only then will it not chase after the phantom of an
historical object which is the object of progressive research, but rather will

learn to see in the object the counterpart of itself and hence understand both'
(266).

12 See Husserl, *Erfahrung und Urteil: Untersuchungen zur Genealogie der Logik*,
trans. *Experience and Judgment: Investigations in a Genealogy of Logic*: 'All
predicative self-evidence must be ultimately grounded on the self-evidence of
experience ... The retrogression to the world of experience is a retrogression to the *life-world*, i.e., to the world in which we are always already living
and which furnishes the ground for all cognitive performance and all
scientific determination' (41).

13 Being-in-the-world (*In-der-Welt-sein*), as I understand it, means the *capacity*
that human beings have *a priori* to have relationships both with things and
with other human beings. I cite from *Sein und Zeit*, trans. *Being and Time*: 'In
understanding a context of relations such as we have mentioned, Dasein
has assigned itself to an *in-order-to*, and it has done so in terms of a
potentiality-for-Being for the sake of which it itself is one which it may have
seized upon either explicitly or tacitly, and which may be either authentic
or inauthentic' (119). This statement was Heidegger's response to the question he had just asked: 'And what is that wherein *Dasein* as Being-in-the-
World understands itself pre-ontologically?'

14 See Ricoeur, *The Rule of Metaphor*, 297–300.

15 I am greatly indebted to my colleague F.E. Sparshott for his clarity in arguing
these issues. His book *The Concept of Criticism* is one of the finest training
manuals for anyone seeking to work out a theoretical argument on the nature
of criticism.

CHAPTER THREE: DERRIDA AND THE MEANING OF THE LITERARY TEXT

1 The first draft of this chapter was written in response to three lectures offered
at the University of Toronto in October of 1979 by Jacques Derrida. The
title of the lecture series was 'Derrida on Language.' The lectures have been
published only in part as 'La Loi du Genre / The Law of Genre' in *Glyph 7*.
The English translation was reprinted in *Critical Inquiry* 7, no 1 (Autumn
1980): 55–82.

   The books by Derrida that I have used in preparing this chapter are the
following: Husserl, *L'Origine de la géométrie* (1962), trans. *Edmund Husserl's
Origin of Geometry: An Introduction. Jacques Derrida*; *De la grammatologie* (1967),
trans. *Of Grammatology*; *La Voix et le phénomène* (1967), trans. *Speech and
Phenomena*; *L'Ecriture et la Différence* (1967), trans. *Writing and Difference*; *La
Dissémination* (1972), trans. *Dissemination*.

2 The analogy to a magnetic field was suggested by A. Gelley in his review
article on *Of Grammatology* in *Diacritics* (Spring 1972): 9–13.

CHAPTER FOUR: RICOEUR AND SHARED MEANING OF INTERPRETATION

1 Richard Rorty, in *Philosophy and the Mirror of Nature*, has clearly challenged the validity of holding up some privileged set of descriptions as the objective truth about the subject at hand. The pertinence of the argument to literary criticism is obvious. See 377–8.
2 The paradigm for this introduction is taken from Ricoeur's 'What is a Text? Explanation and Understanding,' in *Hermeneutics and the Human Sciences*, 145–69. The original publication was 'Qu'est-ce qu'un texte? expliquer et comprendre,' in *Hermeneutik und Dialektik*, vol. 2 (Tübingen: J.C.B. Mohr 1970), 181–200.
3 See Ricoeur, 'What is a Text? Explanation and Understanding,' *Hermeneutics and the Human Sciences*, 158: 'the interpretation of a text culminates in the self-interpretation of a subject who thenceforth understands himself better, understands himself differently or simply begins to understand himself.' See also Rorty, *Philosophy and the Mirror of Nature*, 377: '[Edifying philosophy is] a protest against attempts to close off conversation by proposals for universal commensuration through the hypostatization of some privileged set of descriptions. The danger which edifying discourse tries to avert is that some given vocabulary, some way in which people might come to think of themselves, will deceive them into thinking that from now on all discourse could be, or should be, normal discourse. The resulting freezing-over of culture would be, in the eyes of edifying philosophers, the dehumanization of human beings.'
4 See Ricoeur's 'Appropriation,' in *Hermeneutics and the Human Sciences*, 182–93. This essay is the basic premise for the development of what I have called phenomenological hermeneutics; see especially 'The heuristic fiction as play,' 186–90.
5 See Leech, 'On Seeing a Play,' especially 216.
6 The work of Wolfgang Iser, *The Implied Reader* (1974) and *The Act of Reading* (1978), and Hans Robert Jauss, *Toward an Aesthetic of Reception* (1982) and *Aesthetic Experience and Literary Hermeneutics* (1982), is well established as the theoretical base of reader-reception criticism, but what has not been fully articulated until now is the relation of their work to the phenomenological hermeneutics of Paul Ricoeur. The second volume of *Temps et Récit* (1985) addresses this problem.

CHAPTER FIVE: THE ONTOLOGICAL STATUS OF THE CRITICAL TEXT

1 The source of these observations on the rejection of the opposites of absolute other and absolute self is Paul Ricoeur's 'Hermeneutics and the Critique of

Ideology,' in *Hermeneutics and the Human Sciences*, 63–100; the specific passage in question is on 75.

2 R.G. Collingwood's penetrating study of Croce's *Teoria e Storia della Storiografia* (1917) clearly exposes the tensions between philosophy and history that I have identified as the foundations of Hispanic studies. See Collingwood, 'Croce's Philosophy of History,' in *Essays in the Philosophy of History*, 3–22.

CHAPTER SIX: THE CODA OF *PIEDRA DE SOL*

1 I have previously studied the poem (see 'En busca de la realidad poética' and 'Mito y realidad en *Piedra de Sol*'). The theoretical foundation of the criticism presented in this chapter is based on the writings of Paul Ricoeur. The argument on poetic reference is mine, but all who know Ricoeur's philosophy will readily recognize the extent to which I am indebted to this philosopher. The commentary on the 'gain in meaning' at the centre of his concept of metaphor can be found in *The Rule of Metaphor*, 65–100, 173–216, and summed up on 295–303. See especially 297: 'The gain in meaning is thus inseparable from the productive assimilation through which it is schematized.'

2 The discussion on the relation of action to the poetic text can be examined in 'The Model of the Text: Meaningful Action Considered as a Text,' in *Hermeneutics and the Human Sciences*, 197–221.

Sources and References

Adorno, Theodor W. *Noten zur Literatur*. Frankfurt: Suhrkamp 1960. Trans. M.
Sacristan, *Notas de Literatura*. Barcelona: Ariel 1962
– *Ästhetische Theorie*. Frankfurt: Suhrkamp 1970. Trans. M. Jiménez, *Théorie es-
thétique*. Paris: Klincksieck 1974
Alazraki, Jaime. *Jorge Luis Borges*. New York: Columbia University Press 1971
– 'Oxymoronic Structure in Borges' Essays,' in *The Cardinal Points of Borges*. Ed.
Lowell Dunham and Ivar Ivask. Norman, Oklahoma: University of Oklahoma
Press 1971. 47–53
Altieri, Charles. 'The Hermeneutics of Literary Indeterminacy. A Dissent from
the New Orthodoxy.' *New Literary History* 10, no 1 (1978): 71–100
Anscombe, G.E.M. *Intention*. Oxford: Blackwell 1958
Arendt, Hannah. *The Human Condition*. New York: Doubleday 1959
Arnold, Matthew. *Essays in Criticism. First Series*. Ed. Sister T.M. Hoctor. Chicago:
University of Chicago Press 1968
Bachelard, Gaston. *La Poétique de l'espace*. Paris: Presses Universitaires de
France 1958. Trans. Maria Jolas, *The Poetics of Space*. Boston: Beacon Press
1969
Bannan, John F. *The Philosophy of Merleau-Ponty*. New York: Harcourt, Brace and
World 1967
Barthes, Roland. *Le Degré zéro de l'écriture*. Paris: Seuil 1953. Trans. A. Lavers and
C. Smith, *Writing Degree Zero*. London: Cape 1967
– *Eléments de sémiologie*. Paris: Seuil 1964. Trans. A. Lavers and C. Smith,
Elements of Semiology. London: Cape 1967
– *S/Z*. Paris: Seuil 1970. Trans. R. Miller, *S/Z*. London: Hill and Wang 1974
Bataillon, Marcel. *Erasme et l'Espagne*. Paris: Presses Universitaires de France
1937. Trans. and enlarged edn by Antonio Alatorre, *Erasmo y España*. México:
Fondo de Cultura Económica 1950, 1966

Benveniste, Émile. *Problèmes de linguistique générale*. Paris: Gallimard 1966. Trans. Juan Almela, *Problemas de lingüistica general*. México: Siglo Veintiuno 1971

Blanco Aguinaga, Carlos. *Unamuno teórico del lenguaje*. México: Fondo de Cultura Económica 1954

Bloom, Harold. *The Anxiety of Influence*. New York: Oxford University Press 1973

Bonilla y San Martin, Adolfo. *Luis Vives y la filosofia del renacimiento*. Madrid: Luis Rubio 1929

Borges, Jorge Luis. 'La secta del Fénix,' in *Ficciones*. Buenos Aires: Emecé, 1956. 181–5. Trans. James E. Irby, 'The Sect of the Phoenix,' in *Labryinths: Selected Stories and Other Writings by Jorge Luis Borges*. Ed. Donald A. Yates and James E. Irby. New York: New Directions 1962. 101–4

Bruner, Jerome. *Processes of Cognitive Growth*. Oxford: Clarendon Press 1968

Buck, Günther. 'The Structure of Hermeneutic Experience and the Problem of Tradition,' *New Literary History* 10, no 1 (1978): 31–48

Camponigri, A. Robert. *Time and Idea: The Theory of History in Giambattista Vico*. London: Routledge and Kegan Paul 1953

Cassirer, Ernst. *The Logic of the Humanities*. New Haven: Yale University Press 1960

Collingwood, R.G. *Outlines of a Philosophy of Art*. London: Oxford University Press 1925

– *An Essay on Philosophical Method*. Oxford: Clarendon Press 1933

– *Principles of Art*. Oxford: Clarendon Press 1938

– *The Idea of History*. London: Oxford University Press 1956

– *Essays in the Philosophy of History*. Austin: University of Texas Press 1965. See espec. 'Croce's Philosophy of History,' 3–22, reprinted from *Hibbert Journal* (1921): 263–78.

Croce, Benedetto. *Teoria e storia della storiografia*. Bari: Laterza 1917. Trans. D. Ainsle, *History; Its Theory and Practice*. New York: Russell and Russell 1960

– *La poesia: Introduzione alla Critica e storia della poesia e della letteratura*. 5th edn. Bari: Laterza 1971.

– *Estética como ciencia de la expresión y lingüistica*. Trans. Ángel Vegue y Goldoni, prologue Miguel de Unamuno. Madrid: Beltran 1926

– *La filosofia di Giambattista Vico*. Bari: Laterza 1953

Culler, Jonathan. *Structuralist Poetics*. Ithaca: Cornell University Press 1975

– *The Pursuit of Signs*. Ithaca: Cornell University Press 1981

– *On Deconstruction*. Ithaca: Cornell University Press 1982

De George, Richard, and Fernande, eds. *The Structuralists from Marx to Lévi-Strauss*. New York: Doubleday 1972

de Man, Paul. *Blindness and Insight*. New York: Oxford University Press 1971

– *Allegories of Reading*. New Haven: Yale University Press 1979

Derrida, Jacques. *Edmund Husserl: L'Origine de la géométrie*. Paris: Presses Universitaires de France 1962. Trans. John P. Leavey, *Edmund Husserl's Origin of Geometry: An Introduction*. Stony Brook: Nicolas Hay 1978

- *L'Ecriture et la Différence*. Paris: Seuil 1967. Trans. A. Bass, *Writing and Difference*. Chicago: University of Chicago Press 1978
- *La Voix et le Phénomène*. Paris: Presses Universitaires de France 1967. Trans. D.B. Allison, *Speech and Phenomena*. Evanston: Northwestern University Press 1973
- *De la grammatologie*. Paris: Editions de Minuit 1967. Trans. G. Chakravorty Spivak, *Of Grammatology*. Baltimore: Johns Hopkins University Press 1976
- 'La Pharmacie de Platon.' *Tel Quel* 32, 33 (1968). Also in *La Dissémination*. Paris: Seuil 1972. Trans. Barbara Johnson, *Dissemination*. Chicago: University of Chicago Press 1981. 65–171
- 'La Mythologie blanche.' *Poétique* 5 (1971): 1–52. Also in *Marges de la philosophie*. Paris: Editions de Minuit 1972. Trans. F.C.T. Moore, *New Literary History* 6, no 1 (1974): 5–74. Also trans. Alan Bass, *Margins of Philosophy*. Chicago: University of Chicago Press 1982. 207–72.
- 'La Loi du genre / The Law of Genre.' *Glyph* 7 (1980): 176–232. Trans. Avital Ronell, in *Critical Inquiry* 7, no 1 (Autumn 1980): 55–82
- 'Sending: On Representation.' *Social Research* 49, no 2 (1982): 294–326

Dewey, John. *Art as Experience*. New York: Minton 1934

Dilthey, Wilhelm. 'The Rise of Hermeneutics.' Trans. F. Jameson, *New Literary History* 3, no 2 (1972): 229–44

Doležel, Lubomir. *Narrative Modes in Czech Literature*. Toronto: University of Toronto Press 1973

Eliade, Mircea. *The Sacred and the Profane*. New York: Harcourt, Brace and World 1959

Erlich, Victor. *Russian Formalism: History-Doctrine*. The Hague: Mouton 1965

- *Twentieth-Century Russian Literary Criticism*. New Haven: Yale University Press 1975

Fish, Stanley. *Is There a Text in This Class?* Cambridge, Mass.: Harvard University Press 1980

Frazer, James George. *The Golden Bough: A Study in Magic and Religion*. Abridged edn. New York: Macmillan 1951

Gadamer, Hans Georg. *Wahrheit und Methode*. Tübingen: Mohr 1960. Trans. *Truth and Method*. New York: Seabury Press 1975

- *Hegels Dialektik: fünf hermeneutische Studien*. Tübingen: Mohr 1971. Trans. P. Christopher Smith, *Hegel's Dialectic: Five Hermeneutical Studies*. New Haven: Yale University Press 1976
- *Philosophical Hermeneutics*. Trans. and ed. David E. Linge. Berkeley and Los Angeles: University of California Press 1976
- *Dialogue and Dialectic*. Trans. and ed. P. Christopher Smith. New Haven: Yale University Press 1980

- *Reason in the Age of Science*. Trans. and ed. F.G. Lawrence. Cambridge, Mass.: MIT Press 1982

Gaos, José. *Introducción a 'El ser y el tiempo' de Martin Heidegger*. México: Fondo de Cultura Económica 1951

Greimas, A.J. *Sémantique structurale recherche de méthode*. Paris: Larousse 1966
- *Du sens. Essais sémiotiques*. Paris: Seuil 1970
- ed. *Sign, Language, Culture*. The Hague: Mouton 1970

Grice, Paul. 'Meaning.' *Philosophical Review* 66 (1957): 377–88
- 'Utterer's Meaning.' *Foundations of Language* 4 (1968): 225–45. Also in *Philosophical Review* 78 (1969): 147–77

Guillén, Jorge. *Language and Poetry*. Cambridge, Mass.: Harvard University Press 1961. Trans. *Lenguaje y poesia*. Madrid: Revista de Occidente 1962

Hawkes, Terence. *Structuralism and Semiotics*. Berkeley: University of California Press 1977

Hegel, G.W.F. *The Phenomenology of Mind*. Trans. J.B. Baillie. New York: Harper and Row 1967

Heidegger, Martin. *Sein und Zeit*. Halle: Jahrbuch für philosophische und phäno-menologische Forschung 1927. Trans. José Gaos, *El ser y el tiempo*. México City: Fondo de Cultura Económica 1951. Trans. John Macquarrie and Edward Robinson, *Being and Time*. New York: Harper and Row 1962
- *Existence and Being*. Ed. Werner Brock. Chicago: Henry Regnery 1949. Contains 'Remembrance of the poet,' trans. Douglas Scott; 'Hölderlin and the Essence of Poetry,' trans. Douglas Scott; 'On the Essence of Truth,' trans. R.F.C. Hull and Alan Crick; 'What is Metaphysics,' trans. R.F.C. Hull and Alan Crick.
- *The Question of Being*. Bilingual edn. Trans. W. Kluback and J.T. Wilde. New York: Twayne 1958
- *Der Ursprung des Kunstwerkes*. Ed. H.G. Gadamer. Stuttgart: Reclam 1960
- *Poetry, Language, Thought*. Ed. and trans. Albert Hofstadter. New York: Harper and Row 1971
- *Basic Writings*. Ed. David Farrell Krell. New York: Harper and Row 1977. Contains nine essays and the introduction to *Sein und Zeit*. Five of the essays are not contained in the previously cited collections: 'Letter on Humanism,' trans. Frank A. Capuzzi and J. Glenn Gray; 'Modern Science, Metaphysics and Mathematics,' trans. W.B. Barton and Vera Deutsch; 'The Question concerning Technology,' trans. William Lovitt; 'What Calls for Thinking?' trans. F.D. Wieck and J. Glenn Gray; 'The End of Philosophy and the Task of Thinking,' trans. Joan Stambaugh.

Hernadi, Paul, ed. *What Is Criticism?* Bloomington: Indiana University Press 1981

Hirsch, Eli. *The Concept of Identity*. Oxford University Press 1982

Humboldt, Wilhelm von. *Humanist without Portfolio: An Anthology of the Writings of Wilhem von Humboldt*. Detroit: Wayne State University Press 1963
– *Studienausgabe: Ästhetik und Literatur*. Ed. Kurt Müller-Vollmer. Frankfurt: Fischer-Bücherei 1970
Husserl, Edmund. *Experience and Judgement: Investigations in A Genealogy of Logic*. Trans. K. Ameriks. Evanston: Northwestern University Press 1973
Hutcheon, Linda. *Narcissistic Narrative*. Waterloo, Ont.: Wilfrid Laurier Press 1980; 2nd edn, London: Metheun 1984
Iser, Wolfgang. *The Implied Reader: Patterns of Communication in Prose Fiction from Bunyan to Beckett*. Baltimore: Johns Hopkins University Press 1974
– *The Act of Reading: A Theory of Aesthetic Response*. Baltimore: Johns Hopkins University Press 1978
– 'Narrative Strategies as a Means of Communication.' In *Interpretation of Narrative*. Ed. M.J. Valdés and O.J. Miller. Toronto: University of Toronto Press 1978. 100–17
Jakobson, Roman. 'Linguistics and poetics.' In *The Structuralists from Marx to Lévi-Strauss*. Ed. Richard and Fernande De George. New York: Doubleday 1972. 85–122
Jakobson, Roman, and Claude Lévi-Strauss. 'Charles Baudelaire's *Les chats*.' In *The Structuralists from Marx to Lévi-Strauss*. 124–46
Jameson, Fredric. *The Prison House of Language: A Critical Account of Structuralism and Russian Formalism*. Princeton: Princeton University Press 1972
Jauss, Hans Robert. *Kleine Apologie der ästhetischen Erfahrung*. Konstanz: Konstanzer Universitätsreden 1972
– 'Theses on the Transition from the Aesthetics of Literary Works to a Theory of Aesthetic Experience.' In *Interpretation of Narrative*. Ed. M.J. Valdés and O.J. Miller. Toronto: University of Toronto Press 1978. 137–47
– *Toward an Aesthetic of Reception*. Minneapolis: University of Minnesota Press 1982
– *Aesthetic Experience and Literary Hermeneutics*. Minneapolis: University of Minnesota Press 1982
Johnson, Roberta. 'The Genesis of Gabriel Miro's Ideas about Being and Language: The Barcelona Period 1914–1920.' *Revista Canadiense de Estudios Hispánicos* 8, no 2 (1984): 183–206
Kierkegaard, Søren. *Either/Or*. Trans. W. Lowrie. Garden City: Anchor Books 1959
Kristeller, Paul Oskar. *Renaissance Thought*. New York: Harper and Row 1961
Lanigan, Richard L. *Speaking and Semiology. Maurice Merleau-Ponty's Phenomenological Theory of Existential Communication*. The Hague: Mouton 1972
Leach, Edmund. *Lévi-Strauss*. London: Fontana 1970

Leech, Clifford. 'On Seeing a Play.' In *The Dramatist's Experience*. London: Chatto and Windus 1970. 197–216

Lemon, Lee, and Marion Reis, eds. *Russian Formalist Criticism: Four Essays*. Lincoln: University of Nebraska Press 1965

Lévi-Strauss, Claude. *La Pensée sauvage*. Paris: Plon 1962. Trans., *The Savage Mind*. Chicago: University of Chicago Press 1966

– *Anthropologie structurale*. Paris: Plon 1958. Trans. C. Jacobson and B.G. Schoepf, *Structural Anthropology*. London: Allen Lane 1968

Lida, María Rosa. *Two Spanish Masterpieces. The Book of Good Love and The Celestina*. Urbana: University of Illinois Press 1961

Lotman, Jurij. *The Structure of the Artistic Text*. Trans. Gail Lenhoff and Ronald Vroon. Ann Arbor: Michigan Slavic Contributions, University of Michigan 1977

McLuhan, Marshall, and Harley Parker. *Through the Vanishing Point*. New York: Harper and Row 1968

Mallin, Samuel B. *Merleau-Ponty's Philosophy*. New Haven: Yale University Press 1979

Martínez Bonati, Félix. *La estructura de la obra literaria. Una investigación de filosofía del lenguaje y estética*. Santiago de Chile: Ediciones de la Universidad de Chile 1960; 2nd enlarged edn, Barcelona: Seix Barral 1972. Trans., *Fictive Discourse and the Structures of Literature*. Ithaca: Cornell University Press 1981

– 'Hermeneutic Criticism and the Description of Form.' In *Interpretation of Narrative*. Ed. M.J. Valdés and O.J. Miller. Toronto: University of Toronto Press 1978. 78–99

– 'The Stability of Literary Meaning.' In *Identity of the Literary Text*. Ed. M.J. Valdés and O.J. Miller. Toronto: University of Toronto Press 1985. 231–45

Matejka, Ladislav, and Krystina Pomorska, eds. *Readings in Russian Poetics: Formalist and Structuralist Views*. Cambridge, Mass.: MIT Press 1971

Merleau-Ponty, Maurice. *The Primacy of Perception*. Ed. James M. Edie. Evanston: Northwestern University Press 1964. See espec. 'Le Primat de la perception et ses conséquences philosophiques' (1945), trans. James M. Edie, 'The Primacy of Perception and Its Philosophical Consequences,' 12–42.

– *Phénoménologie de la perception*. Paris: Gallimard 1946. Trans. Colin Smith, *Phenomenology of Perception*. London: Routledge and Kegan Paul 1962

– *Signes*. Paris: Gallimard 1960. Trans. R.G. McCleary, *Signs*. Evanston: Northwestern University Press 1964. See espec. 'On the Phenomenology of Language,' 84–97.

– *Sens et Non-sens*. 2nd edn. Paris: Éditions Nagel 1961. Trans. H.L. Dreyfus and P.A. Dreyfus, *Sense and Non-Sense*. Evanston: Northwestern University Press 1964. See espec. 'Metaphysics and the Novel,' 26–40.

- *L'Oeil et l'Esprit*. Paris: Gallimard 1964. First published in *Art de France* 1, no 1 (1961). Trans. Carleton Dallery in *The Primacy of Perception and Other Essays*. Ed. James M. Edie. Evanston: Northwestern University Press 1964
- *Résumés de cours, Collège de France 1952–60*. Paris: Gallimard 1968. Trans. John O'Neill, *Themes from the Lectures at the Collège de France*. Evanston: Northwestern University Press 1970. See espec. 'Studies in the Literary Use of Language,' 12–18.
- *Le Visible et l'Invisible*. Paris: Gallimard 1964. Trans. Alphonso Lingis, *The Visible and The Invisible*. Evanston: Northwestern University Press 1968
- *La Prose du monde*. Paris: Gallimard 1969. Trans. John O'Neill, *The Prose of the World*. Evanston: Northwestern University Press 1973. See espec. 'Dialogue and the Perception of the Other,' 131–146.
- Missenard, André. *A la recherche de l'homme*. Trans. L.G. Blochman, *In Search of Man*. New York: Hawthorn Books 1957
- Müller-Vollmer, Kurt. *Towards a Phenomenological Theory of Literature: A Study of Wilhelm Dilthey's Poetik*. The Hague: Mouton 1963
- Murray, Michael, ed. *Heidegger and Modern Philosophy*. New Haven: Yale University Press 1978
- Noreña, Carlos. *Juan Luis Vives*. The Hague: Martinus Nijhoff 1970
- Paz, Octavio. *El arco y la lira*. México City: Fondo de Cultura Económica 1956
- *Piedra de sol*. In *Libertad bajo palabra: obra poética 1935–1957*. México City: Fondo de Cultura Económica 1960
- *Corriente alterna*. México City: Siglo Veintiuno 1967
- *Claude Lévi-Strauss o el nuevo festín de Esopo*. México City: Joaquin Mortiz 1967
- *Los hijos de limo*. Barcelona: Seix Barral 1974
- *In/mediaciones*. Barcelona: Seix Barral 1979
- *Sombras de obras*. Barcelona: Seix Barral 1983
- Pellauer, David. 'The Significance of the Text in Paul Ricoeur's Hermeneutical Theory.' In *Studies in the Philosophy of Paul Ricoeur*. Athens: Ohio University Press 1979. 97–114
- Pettit, Philip. *The Concept of Structuralism*. London: Gill and MacMillan 1976
- Piaget, Jean. *Le Structuralisme*. Paris: Presses Universitaires de France 1968. Trans. C. Maschler, *Structuralism*. London: Routledge and Kegan Paul 1971
- Pöggler, Otto. 'Being as Appropriation.' In *Heidegger and Modern Philosophy*. Ed. M. Murray. New Haven: Yale University Press 1978. 84–115
- Reagan, Charles E., ed. *Studies in the Philosophy of Paul Ricoeur*. Athens: Ohio University Press 1979
- Ricoeur, Paul. 'Le Symbolisme et l'explication structurale.' *Cahiers Internationales de Symbolisme* 4 (1964): 81–96
- *Le Conflict des interprétations*. Paris: Seuil 1969. Trans. *The Conflict of Interpreta-*

tions: Essays in Hermeneutics. Ed. Don Ihde. Evanston: Northwestern University Press 1974
- 'The Hermeneutical Function of Distanciation.' *Philosophy Today* 17 (1973): 129–41
- *La Métaphore vive*. Paris: Seuil 1975. Trans. Robert Czerny, Kathleen McLaughlin, and John Costello, *The Rule of Metaphor: Multi-disciplinary Studies of the Creation of Meaning in Language*. Toronto: University of Toronto Press 1977
- *Interpretation Theory: Discourse and the Surplus of Meaning*. Fort Worth: Texas Christian University 1976
- *The Philosophy of Paul Ricoeur: An Anthology of His Work*. Ed. Charles Reagan and David Stewart. Boston: Beacon Press 1978. See espec. 'Existence and Hermeneutics,' 97–108; 'Structure, Word, Event,' 109–19; 'Creativity in Language,' 120–33; 'Metaphor and the Main Problem of Hermeneutics,' 134–48; and 'Explanation and Understanding,' 149–66.
- *Hermeneutics and the Human Sciences. Essays on Language, Action and Interpretation*. Ed. and trans. John R. Thompson. Cambridge: Cambridge University Press 1981. See especially 'The Task of Hermeneutics,' 43–62; 'Hermeneutics and the Critique of Ideology,' 63–100; 'Phenomenology and Hermeneutics,' 101–30; 'The Hermeneutical Function of Distanciation,' 131–44; 'What Is a Text? Explanation and Understanding,' 154–64; 'Appropriation,' 182–96; 'The Model of the Text: Meaningful Action Considered as Text,' 197–221; 'The Narrative Function,' 274–96.
- *Temps et Récit*. Vols. 1–3. Paris: Seuil 1983–85
Riffaterre, Michael. 'The Reader's Perception of Narrative: Balzac's *Paix du ménage*.' In *Interpretation of Narrative*. Ed. M.J. Valdés and O.J. Miller. Toronto: University of Toronto Press 1978. 28–38
- *Semiotics of Poetry*. Bloomington: Indiana University Press 1978
Rorty, Richard. 'Philosophy as a Kind of Writing: An Essay on Derrida.' *New Literary History* 10, no 1 (1978): 141–60
- *Philosophy and the Mirror of Nature*. Princeton: Princeton University Press 1979
Russell, Bertrand. 'On Denoting.' In *Contemporary Readings in Logical Theory*. Ed. I.M. Copi and A. Gould. New York: MacMillan 1967. 93–105
Sapir, Edward. *Language: An Introduction into the Study of Speech*. New York: Harcourt Brace 1921
- *Culture, Language and Personality*. Ed. D.G. Mandelbaum. Berkeley: University of California Press 1957
Saussure, Ferdinand de. *Cours de linguistique générale*. Ed. Tullio de Mauro. Paris: Payot 1960. Trans. Wade Baskin, *Course in General Linguistics*. New York: McGraw-Hill 1966

Saville, Anthony. 'Historicity and the Hermeneutic Circle,' *New Literary History* 10, no 1 (1978): 49–70

Schaldenbrand, Mary. 'Metaphoric Imagination: Kinship Through Conflict.' In *Studies in the Philosophy of Paul Ricoeur*. Ed. Charles E. Reagan. Athens: Ohio University Press 1979. 57–82

Schleiermacher, F.D.E. 'The Hermeneutics: Outline of the 1819 Lectures.' *New Literary History* 10, no 1 (1978): 1–16

Schutz, Alfred. *Der sinnhafte Aufbau der sozialen Welt*. Vienna: Julias Springer 1932. Trans. George Walsh and Frederick Lehnert, *The Phenomenology of the Social World*. Evanston: Northwestern University Press 1967. See especially 'Foundations of a Theory of Intersubjective Understanding,' 97–139

– *On Phenomenology and Social Relations: Selected Writings*. Ed. Helmut R. Wagner. Chicago: University of Chicago Press 1970

Searle, John. *Speech Acts*. Cambridge: Cambridge University Press 1969

Sebeok, Thomas A. *Style in Language*. Cambridge, Mass.: MIT Press 1960

Sparshott, F.E. 'Truth in Fiction.' *Journal of Aesthetics and Art Criticism* 26 (1967): 3–7

– *The Concept of Criticism*. Oxford: Oxford University Press 1967

– 'As: or, The Limits of Metaphor.' *New Literary History* 6, no 1 (1974): 75–94

– 'Goodman on Expression.' *Monist* 58 (1974): 187–202

– 'On the Possibility of a General Theory of Literature.' *Centrum* 3 (1975): 5–22

– 'The Problem of the Problem of Criticism.' In *What Is Criticism?* Ed. Paul Hernadi. Bloomington: Indiana University Press 1981

Steiner, George. *After Babel*. London: Oxford University Press 1975

Strawson, P.F. 'On Referring.' *Mind* 59 (1950): 320–44

Szondi, Peter. 'Introduction to Literary Hermeneutics.' *New Literary History* 10, no 1 (1978): 17–30

Tel Quel: Théorie d'ensemble. Paris: Seuil 1968

Thompson, John B. *Critical Hermeneutics: A Study of the Thought of Paul Ricoeur and Jürgen Habermas*. Cambridge: Cambridge University Press 1981

Tynyanov, Jurij, and Roman Jakobson. 'Problems in the Study of Language and Literature.' In Richard and Fernande De George, *The Structuralists from Marx to Lévi-Strauss*. New York: Doubleday 1972. 80–3

Unamuno, Miguel de. 'Vida del Romance Castellano: Historia de la lengua Española' (inédito, 1900?). In *Obras Completas*, vol. 4. Madrid: Escelicer 1968. 659–92

– *Del sentimiento trágico de la vida en los hombres y los pueblos* (1913). In *Obras Completas*, vol. 7. Madrid: Escelicer 1968. 109–304. Trans. Anthony Kerrigan, *The Tragic Sense of Life in Men and Nations*. Princeton: Princeton University Press 1972

- 'Alrededor del estilo' (1924). In *Obras Completas*, vol. 7. Madrid: Escelicer 1968. 885–950
- 'Notas Marginales' (1925). In *Obras Completas*, vol. 4. Madrid: Escelicer 1968. 698–703
Valdés, Mario J. *Death in the Literature of Unamuno*. Urbana: University of Illinois Press 1964
- 'En busca de una realidad poética: un estudio de *Piedra de sol.*' *Canadian Journal of Latin American Studies* 2 (1977): 259–69
- 'Mito y realidad en *Piedra de sol.*' *Cuadernos de communicación* 2, no 17 (1977): 22–37
- *Shadows in the Cave: A Phenomenological Approach to Literary Criticism Based on Hispanic Texts*. Toronto: University of Toronto Press 1982
Valdés, Mario J., and María Elena de Valdés. *An Unamuno Source Book*. Toronto: University of Toronto Press 1973
Valdés, Mario J., and O.J. Miller, eds. *Interpretation of Narrative*. Toronto: University of Toronto Press 1978
- *Identity of the Literary Text*. Toronto: University of Toronto Press 1985
Valéry, Paul. *Aesthetics*. Ed. Jackson Mathews, trans. Ralph Manheim. New York: Bollingen Foundation and Pantheon Books 1964
Vico, Giambattista. *L'Autobiografia, Il Carteggio, e la Posie Varie*. A cura di Benedetto Croce. Bari: Laterza 1911
- *La Scienza Nuova Prima* (1725). A cura di Fausto Nicolini. Bari: Laterza 1931
- *La Scienza Nuova Seconda* (1744). A cura di Fausto Nicolini. 3rd rev. edn. Bari: Laterza 1928. Trans. T.G. Bergin and M.H. Fisch, *The New Science of Giambattista Vico*. Ithaca: Cornell University Press 1948, 1968, 1984. The 1968 English translation is the revised and unabridged edition, based on the 1744 3rd rev. edn, published with notes by Nicolini in 1928. The 1984 English translation includes 'Practice of the New Science' for the first time.
Vives, Juan Luis. *Obras Completas*. Ed. Lorenzo Riber. 2 vols. Madrid: Aguilar 1947
- *Against the Pseudodialecticians*. Trans. and ed. Rita Guerlac. Dordrecht, Netherlands: D. Reidel 1979
Von Bertalanffy, L. 'An Essay on the Relativity of Categories.' *Philosophy of Science* 22 (1955): 243–63
Weimann, Robert. '"Appropriation" and Modern History in Renaissance Prose Narrative,' *New Literary History* 14, no 3 (1983): 459–96
Whorf, Benjamin Lee. *Language, Thought and Reality: Selected Writings of Benjamin Lee Whorf*. Ed. J.B. Carroll. Cambridge, Mass.: MIT Press 1956
Wittgenstein, Ludwig. *Philosophical Investigations*. Trans. G.E.M. Anscombe. Oxford: Basil Blackwell 1968

Author-Title Index

UNIVERSITY OF TORONTO ROMANCE SERIES